MW00637826

"*Sonna cosa nostra*, these are our affairs.
We will manage our world for ourselves
because it is our world, *cosa nostra*."

MARIO PUZO, *THE GODFATHER*

EDITED BY PAUL DUNCAN

The Godfather Family Album

PHOTOGRAPHS BY
STEVE SCHAPIRO

TASCHEN

THE GODFATHER PART I

THE GODFATHER PART II

THE GODFATHER PART III

Foreword

STEVE SCHAPIRO
CHICAGO, 2008

When I first arrived on the set of *The Godfather* for a scene in New York's Lower East Side, I had already heard the rumors that Marlon Brando was in bad health. The streets and surrounding tenements were teeming with onlookers; even the fire escapes were crammed with children and their grandmothers. Everyone, it seemed, wanted to catch a glimpse of the man who had been chosen to play Don Vito Corleone.

I had convinced *Life* magazine to do a "guaranteed" cover story on the *Godfather* film — something they did not ordinarily do — provided Paramount would grant *Life* the exclusive right to print the photographs before any other publication. Curiosity as to what Brando would look like in the film had already captured the public's imagination, and Paramount's plan was to keep everything as secretive as possible and to hold back on revealing Brando's look until the film actually came out.

As I approached the set, the crew was setting up for the attempted assassination of the don. When I came closer I noticed a sallow-faced elderly man, wearing a worn coat and hat and talking in a low, frail voice to an assistant director. I suddenly realized that I was looking at Marlon Brando. My heart sank, and at that moment I thought all the bad-health rumors must really be true.

Then Brando suddenly turned away, facing the many spectators, and the electricity of a young man's eyes shot out into the crowd. Brando turned back to the AD, and warned in his familiar dynamic voice, "Someone's out there with a camera." It was not until the farewell party, after production was finished, that I saw the real Marlon Brando — a smiling, handsome man in his 40s who had just accomplished one of the greatest tours de force in the world of acting.

It is common knowledge that, at the time, no one thought this film would be an important film — or even a good one. It was rumored that Paramount executives were sending out their secretaries during lunchtime to buy copies of Mario Puzo's novel, hoping the increased sales might influence the *New York Times* best-seller list and heighten public interest.

It was uncertain whether there would be enough funding available to finish shooting, and days were removed from the shooting schedule because of the tight budget. The controversy had begun with casting and continued through every turn of the wheel. During the filming itself, there were days when I saw director Francis Ford Coppola unable to capture the respect — or even, it seemed, the attention — of some of his own assistant directors.

What emerged was not the two-dimensional New York gangster picture it might have been. Francis carefully chose the actors for their inner qualities and depth, and then allowed them to cultivate these emotions. As a result, deeper dimensions grew and came to life. The set was filled with humor, from practical jokes to the famous mooning episodes. The Coppola family worked like the Corleone family, and everyone melded together.

Coppola also believed in the importance of props as a means toward authenticity. He knew that if he provided one of his actors with a prop as stimulus, the actor would make something out of it. With that in mind, Francis found a stray cat that had been running around the Filmways Studio and pushed it onto Brando's lap, without comment, and let Brando develop it into what would become an epiphany for Don Corleone's character — and, eventually, the logo for the film.

As a photographer, sometimes you just need to be a fly on the wall. Shooting the movie's opening sequence in Don Corleone's office meant working with a blimp (a metal box, sponge-foamed inside to muffle the still camera's clicks), or waiting until the scene was finished so that it could be replayed for the still camera. My two most memorable images came from within those doors: Brando holding the cat, and Salvatore Corsitto, as Bonasera, whispering into the don's ear. Both photographs have been used over and over again to iconize the movie, and are now familiar images throughout the world.

But there are also times when a photographer has license to shoot at will, looking for the candid moments. The organized chaos of the wedding-party scene offered a wonderful opportunity to capture the actors at work, and at play.

Behind the scenes, all the tricks of the trade are revealed, like the wiring-up of James Caan with gunpowder-filled brass casings and sacs of fake blood — all to be set off by remote control to create the illusion that the bullets are hitting him from a distance, riddling his body with bullet holes and blood.

During the filming of *The Godfather: Part II*, Gordon Willis, the cinematographer, seemed to be going for an Oscar. Usually it was almost noon before he would feel his lighting was ready for the first shot of the day. For a scene on a hotel balcony in the Dominican Republic, where Lee Strasberg sits with Al Pacino to cut the cake that symbolizes Cuba, the light continued to be just not quite right for four days. We remained there, doing the same scene over and over. One morning, I took Al Pacino around the corner of the balcony to do a portrait against a glass window. With some actors, I've had to jump up and down or even make bird sounds to get the appropriate look. Al, within half a roll, had given me anything I could ever ask for, and we were done.

In Sicily, it was like a merger of families — everyone had family there. My fondest memory is of Coppola's mother coming out one morning dressed exactly like Francis — with a false beard, glasses, and the same brown corduroy jacket he always wore. They looked almost identical, together beneath the Corleone town sign.

During a film production, the still and "special" photographers are low men on the totem pole. They are thought to take time and energy away from the production, and their work is considered unessential to the finished film itself. Yet for *The Great Gatsby*, Paramount credited me with making $7 million for the company through my soft, romantic

images, which appeared on many magazine covers and throughout the entire advertising campaign. (The film, though incredibly beautiful, was slow-moving and didn't inspire the necessary word of mouth to become a blockbuster.)

For *The Godfather: Part III*, besides shooting during scenes, my primary assignment was to create a poster to advertise the movie. It was decided while we were in Palermo, Italy, that I would photograph Al Pacino sitting in a hallway, with light streaming through the windows behind him, reflecting onto the floor. Dutifully, we set up for this shot at 9:00 a.m., with that wonderful light just the way I wanted it. And then we waited. And waited. And then we waited some more. The scene being filmed in the study was long, and Al was simply never available. Time continued to pass, and it was five o'clock that afternoon before Al was finally available for the photograph.

By that time, those special rays of light had passed us by. I had a strobe lamp coming from the side to illuminate Al himself, but the only way to light the window and the floor the way we had

planned was to make a four-second timed exposure with the camera. Al Pacino is not exactly the sort of person who likes to sit still in a chair for very long. I would click open the camera shutter, the strobe light would go off — and so would Al. Before we could say anything, he was standing up, in a completely different position. He was double-exposed on the entire first roll of film I took.

Finally, I explained in greater detail what we were up against. We cut back to a three-second exposure, Al sat still, and the photo came out as the poster image we had dreamed of, with hardly any retouching at all.

The Godfather trilogy is a story about love, honor, revenge, violence, family, and the handing down from one generation to the next. It strikes chords in all of us. It was a coming together of script, direction, actors, lighting, costume, and scenic design. I was very fortunate to see all this happen firsthand, along with the behind-the-scenes moments that made it an even more poignant event. I hope this book conveys at least a little bit of what I saw of *The Godfather.*

The Making Of
The Godfather

TEXT BY MARIO PUZO
EXCERPTED FROM *THE GODFATHER PAPERS
AND OTHER CONFESSIONS,* 1972

The real reason I decided to write the piece that follows was, I think, because the wheels at Paramount refused to let me see the final cut of the movie when and how I wanted to see it. I hate to admit I have that much ego, but what the hell, nobody's perfect.

That incident as described also made me come to the decision that I would never write another movie unless I had final say. I so instructed my agent. Which, in practical terms, means I'm out of the movie business.

Before all this happened I signed to write two more movies, which at this time are almost done. So I think I'm qualified to say that the movie script is the least satisfying form for a writer. But, like most everything else, it's fun to try one time.

Most movies are lousy, and they are lousy because the people who have final say really don't know how story and character work. Hollywood still hasn't caught on that it's money in the bank to promote a writer to a status equal to that of producer, director, and (dare I say it) studio chief.

THE BOOK

I have written three novels. *The Godfather* is not as good as the preceding two; I wrote it to make money. My first novel, *The Dark Arena* (1955), received mostly very good reviews saying I was a writer to watch. Naturally I thought I was going to be rich and famous. The book netted me $3,500 and I still didn't know I had a whole 15 years to wait.

My second novel, *The Fortunate Pilgrim*, was published 10 years later (1965) and netted me $3,000. I was going downhill fast. Yet the book received some extraordinarily fine reviews. The *New York Times* called it a "small classic." I even like the book myself and immodestly think of it as art.

Anyway, I was a hero, I thought. But my publisher, Atheneum, known as a classy publishing house more interested in belles lettres

than money, was not impressed. I asked them for an advance to start on my next book (which would be a *big* classic), and the editors were cool. They were courteous. They were kind. They showed me the door.

I couldn't believe it. I went back and read all the reviews on my first two books. (I skipped the bad ones.) There must be some mistake. I was acknowledged as a real talent, at least. Listen, I was a real writer, honest, a genuine artist, two acclaimed novels behind me, every word in them sweated over and all mine. No help from anybody. It couldn't be true that my publisher would not give me an advance for another novel.

Well, we had another talk. The editors didn't like the idea behind my new novel. It sounded like another loser. One editor wistfully remarked that if *The Fortunate Pilgrim* had only had a little more of that Mafia stuff in it maybe the book would have made money. (One of the minor characters was a Mob chief.)

I was 45 years old and tired of being an artist. Besides, I owed $20,000 to relatives, finance companies, banks, and assorted bookmakers and shylocks. It was really time to grow up and sell out, as Lenny Bruce once advised. So I told my editors OK, I'll write a book about the Mafia, just give me some money to get started. They said no money until we see 100 pages. I compromised; I wrote a 10-page outline. They showed me the door again.

There is no way to explain the terrible feeling of rejection, the damage, the depression and weakening of will such manipulation does to a writer. But this incident also enlightened me. I had been naive enough to believe that publishers cared about art. They didn't. They wanted to make money. (Please don't say, "No kidding.") They were in business. They had a capital investment and payrolls to meet. If some lunatic wanted to create a work of art, let him do it on his own time.

I had been a true believer in art. I didn't believe in religion or love or women or men; I didn't believe in society or philosophy. But I

> "The Godfather is the story of a great king who had three sons, and each got a different part of his palace. Michael got his cunning, Sonny his hot temper, and Alfredo his sweetness." — FRANCIS FORD COPPOLA

believed in art for 45 years. It gave me a comfort I found in no other place. But I knew I'd never be able to write another book if the next one wasn't a success. The psychological and economic pressure would be too much. I had never doubted I could write a best-selling commercial novel whenever I chose to do so. My writing friends, my family, my children, and my creditors all assured me now was the time to put up or shut up.

I was willing, I had a 10-page outline — but nobody would take me. Months went by. I was working on a string of adventure magazines, editing, writing freelance stories, and being treated by the publisher, Martin Goodman, better than I had been by any other publisher I had ever had. I was ready to forget novels except maybe as a puttering hobby for my old age. But one day a writer friend dropped in to my magazine office. As a natural courtesy I gave him a copy of *The Fortunate Pilgrim*. A week later he came back. He thought I was a great writer. I bought him a magnificent lunch. During lunch I told him some funny Mafia stories and of my 10-page outline. He was enthusiastic. He arranged a meeting for me with the editors of G. P. Putnam's Sons. The editors just sat around for an hour listening to my Mafia tales and said go ahead. They also gave me a $5,000 advance and I was on my way, just like that. Almost — almost, I believed that publishers were human.

As soon as I got my hands on the Putnam money, I naturally didn't work on the book. (Luckily part of the advance was payable on

Page 12: Marlon Brando tickles the ivories between takes.

Above: Author Mario Puzo on the set of *The Godfather: Part II.*

15

Below: The end of *The Godfather: Part II* featured a flashback scene showing idealistic young Michael Corleone (Al Pacino, right) before he took over the family from his father, and before he killed three of the people in the room.

Tom Hagen (Robert Duvall), Fredo Corleone (John Cazale), Carlo Rizzi (Gianni Russo), director Francis Ford Coppola, Sonny Corleone (James Caan), and Sal Tessio (Abe Vigoda).

the handing in of the complete manuscript or I would never have finished it.) The thing is, I didn't really want to write *The Godfather.* There was another novel I wanted to write. (I never did and now I never will. Subject matter rots like everything else.)

All my fellow editors on the adventure magazine told me to get cracking on the book. They all were sure it would make my fortune. I had all the good stories, it was writing to my strength. Everybody I knew was sure it was the right thing to do and so finally I started. And quit my job.

It took me three years to finish. During that time I wrote three adventure stories a month for Martin Goodman on a freelance basis. I sneaked in a children's book that got a rave review from *The New Yorker* magazine, the first time they knew I was alive, and I wrote a lot of book reviews. Also magazine pieces, two of which were for the *New York Times Sunday Magazine*, who, though they do not stuff your pockets with gold, treat your work with enormous respect. It is also, in my opinion, the best place to appear if you're out to influence our society. Anyway, in those three years I wrote more than in my whole previous life put together. And it was mostly all fun. I remember it as the happiest time of my life. (Family and friends disagree.)

I'm ashamed to admit that I wrote *The Godfather* entirely from research. I never met a real, honest-to-God gangster. I knew the gambling world pretty good, but that's all. After the book became "famous," I was introduced to a few gentlemen related to the material. They were flattering. They refused to believe that I had never been in the rackets. They refused to believe that I had never had the confidence of a don. But all of them loved the book.

In different parts of the country I heard a nice story: that the Mafia had paid me $1 million to write *The Godfather* as a public-relations con. I'm not in the literary world much, but I hear some writers claim I must have been a Mafia man, that the book could not have been written purely out of research. I treasure the compliment.

I finally had to finish *The Godfather* in July 1968 because I needed the final $1,200 advance payment from Putnam to take my wife and kids to Europe. My wife had not seen her family for 20 years, and I had promised her that this was the year. I had no money, but I had a great collection of credit cards. Still, I needed that $1,200 in cash, so I handed in the rough manuscript. Before leaving for Europe, I told my publisher not to show the book to anybody; it had to be polished.

My family had a good time in Europe. American Express offices cash $500 checks against their credit cards. I used their offices in London, Cannes, Nice, and Wiesbaden. My children and I gambled in the poshest casinos on the French Riviera. If just one of us could have gotten lucky, I would have been able to cover those checks that American Express airmailed back to the United States. We all lost. I had failed as a father. When we finally got home, I owed the credit-card companies $8,000. I wasn't worried. If worse came to worst, we could always sell our house. Or I could go to jail. Hell, better writers had gone to jail. No sweat.

I went into New York to see my agent, Candida Donadio. I was hoping she'd pull a slick magazine assignment out of her sleeve and bail me out as she'd often done in the past. She informed me that my publisher had just turned down $375,000 for the paperback rights to *The Godfather.*

I had given strict orders that it wasn't to be shown to even a paperback house, but this was no time to complain. I called my editor at Putnam, Bill Targ, and he said they were holding out for $410,000 because $400,000 was some sort of record. Did I wish to speak to Clyde Taylor, their reprint-rights man, who was handling the negotiations? I said no; I said that I had absolute confidence in any man who could turn down $375,000. I hung around New York, had a very late lunch with Targ, and over our coffee he got a call. Ralph Daigh of Fawcett had bought the paperback rights for $410,000.

I went up to the adventure-magazine office to quit my freelance job and tell all my friends there the good news. We had some drinks and then I decided to get home to Long Island. While waiting for my car, I called my brother to tell him the good news. This brother had 10 percent of *The Godfather* because he supported me all my life and gave me a final chunk of money to complete the book. Through the years I'd call him up frantic for a few hundred bucks to pay the mortgage or buy the kids shoes. Then I'd arrive at his house in a taxi to pick up the money. In rain or snow he never took a taxi, but he never complained. He always came through. So now I wanted him to know that since my half of the paperback rights came to $205,000 (the hardcover publishers keep half), he was in for a little over 20 grand.

He is the kind of guy who is always home when I call to borrow money. Now that I had money to give back, he was naturally out. I got my mother on the phone. She speaks broken English but understands the language perfectly. I explained it to her.

She asked, "$40,000?"

I said no, it was $410,000. I told her three times before she finally answered, "Don't tell nobody." My car came out of the garage and I hung up. Traffic was jammed, and it took me over two hours to get home out in the suburbs. When I walked in the door, my wife was dozing over the TV and the kids were all out playing. I went over to my wife, kissed her on the cheek, and said, "Honey, we don't have to worry about money anymore. I just sold my book for $410,000."

She smiled at me and kept dozing. I went down to my workroom to call my brothers and sisters. The reason for this was because every Italian family has a "chooch" (a donkey). That is, a family idiot everybody agrees will never be able to make a living and so has to be helped without rancor or reproach. I was the family "chooch," and I just wanted to tell them I was abdicating the family role.

I called my older sister.

"Did you hear?" I said.

My sister's voice was pretty cool. I started getting annoyed. Nobody seemed to think

this was a big deal. My whole life was going to change; I didn't have to worry about money. It was almost like not having to worry about dying. Then my sister said, "You got $40,000 for the book. Mama called me."

I was exasperated with my mother. After all those explanations she had gotten it wrong. Her 80 years were no excuse. "No," I told my sister, "it was $410,000."

Now I got the reaction I wanted. There was a little scream over the phone and an excited minute of conversation. But I had to get back to my mother. I called and said, "Ma, how the hell could you get it wrong? I told you five times that it was $410,000, not $40,000. How could you make such a mistake?"

There was a long silence and then my mother whispered over the phone, "I no maka a mistake. I don't wanta tell her."

When I got through with all the phone calls, my wife was in bed asleep. So were the kids. I went to bed and slept like a rock. When I woke up the next morning, my wife and kids circled the

"Anything you build on a large scale or with intense passion invites chaos."
—FRANCIS FORD COPPOLA

bed. My wife said, "What was that you said last night?" She had just grasped the whole thing.

Well, it's a nice happy ending. But nobody seemed to believe me. So I called Bill Targ and drew an advance check for $100,000. I paid my debts, paid my agents' commissions, paid my brother his well-deserved 10 percent, and three months later I called my publishers and agent for more money. They were stunned. What about the huge check I had just gotten three months before? I couldn't resist. Why should I treat them any differently than I had treated my family all those lean years? "A hundred grand doesn't last forever," I said.

At least I could be a publisher's "chooch."

The Godfather to date had earned over $1 million, but I still wasn't rich. Some of the money was diverted to trust funds for the kids. There were agents' commissions and lawyers' fees. There were federal and state income taxes. All of which cut the original million to less than half. But before I grasped all this I had a great time. I spent the money as fast as it came in. The only thing was that I felt very unnatural being out of debt. I didn't owe anybody one penny.

I loved the money, but I didn't really like being "famous." I found it quite simply distressing. I never much liked parties, never liked talking to more than two or three people at one time. I dislike interviews and having my picture taken (with reason).

I got conned into doing the TV *Today Show* by an editor at Putnam's saying, "How do you know you don't like it when you've never done

Opposite: The Corleone women and children dutifully wait for their husbands, sons, and fathers to return home, never having an active part of the family business. At left: Mama Corleone (Morgana King) and Connie Corleone (Talia Shire).

Above: Director Francis Ford Coppola dictating notes during a break between setups.

> "I was getting 'fired' every other week. The things they were going to fire me over were, one: wanting to cast Brando. Two: wanting to cast Pacino. Wanting to shoot in Sicily; wanting to make it in period. The very things that made the film different from any other film." — FRANCIS FORD COPPOLA

Above: There were many practical jokes during filming, and a lot of mooning from James Caan, Robert Duvall, and Marlon Brando.

it?" That sounded reasonable. I did it. I hated it. So I was never tempted when offers came from the other talk shows. I don't think it was a reverse snobbism. Or a phony kind of humility. It's just damn uncomfortable. And nearly every writer I've seen on TV has seemed foolish; it's not a writer's medium.

Interviews came out sounding like someone I didn't even know; and I couldn't even blame the interviewers. I did make those dumb statements, but I didn't say them like *that*. So I quit going on TV and all publicity, including interviews. And, thank God, I never went on those cross-country trips that are supposed to help a book to best-sellerdom. Not because of other people but because of me. To meet a strange person is always a shock to my nervous system, but I think that's true of most people.

In the meantime I had made what turned out to be a very big mistake. Just before *The*

Godfather was finished, I sold the paperback rights of *The Fortunate Pilgrim* for a $1,500 cash advance against the usual royalties. I sold them to Lancer Books, and one of the partners, Irwin Stein, was so agreeable he sent me the $1,500 in one whole payment rather than reserving half for the publication date.

A bigger mistake was made long before publication when I had the first 100 pages of *The Godfather* done. The William Morris Agency approved a contract with Paramount for the book for a $12,500 option payment, against $50,000, with "escalators" *if* they exercised the option. I had already switched to Candida Donadio as agent, but William Morris had signed the initial book contract and so represented me in the movie deal. They advised me against taking it. They advised me to wait. That was like advising a guy underwater to take a deep breath. I needed the cash and the $12,500 looked like Fort Knox. Let me say now that the fault was mine. But I never held it against Paramount that they got *The Godfather* so cheap.

Now all through this chapter I'll mention how people did things that seem like sharp practice, and the reader may get the impression that I resent it or was surprised or offended. Never. In the world and society we live in almost all these actions were perfectly reasonable. The fact that I feel that the William Morris Agency might have sold me down the river to Paramount Pictures does not mean that I disapprove, condemn, or even am resentful. I consider it perfectly reasonable business behavior on their part.

Anyway, to wind up. *The Godfather* became the number one best seller in the USA; 67 weeks on the *New York Times* list; also number one in England, France, Germany, and other countries. It's been translated into 17 or 20 languages; I stopped keeping track. They tell me it's the fastest- and best-selling fiction paperback of all time or will be when the new "film edition" comes with the movie — but one can't believe everything publishers tell their authors. Though Ralph Daigh at Fawcett proved a straight guy

and promoted the book like hell. Even paid me everything he said I sold. It's a success all right, and I remember one day when I was working on it. My wife sent me to the supermarket; my daughter asked me to drive her to her girlfriend's; my son wanted a ride to football practice. I exploded. I said, "Jesus Christ, do you guys know I'm working on a book that could make me $100,000?" They looked at me and we all laughed together.

The book got much better reviews than I expected. I wished like hell I'd written it better. I like the book. It has energy and I lucked out by creating a central character that was popularly accepted as genuinely mythic. But I wrote below my gifts in that book.

THE MOVIE

I had read the literature about Hollywood, how they did in Fitzgerald, Nathanael West, and novelists in general.

I had already had one enlightening experience with Hollywood movie producers. Earlier that year my agent had called to ask that I come to New York to meet John Foreman, who produces most of the Paul Newman movies. I live 50 miles out in the suburbs and hate New York. But my agent said that John Foreman had read *The Fortunate Pilgrim*, was in love with the book, and wanted to make it a movie. He was a big wheel. I really should make the trip.

I did and it was worth it. John Foreman talked for three hours about my book, how he loved it, how he was determined to do it as a movie. He quoted all the best parts. He liked all the right things. I was thrilled and impressed. The movie was definitely on. As he left, he said he would call my agent the next day and arrange the financial details of the contract.

Nobody ever heard from him again.

So I was not interested at all in what Hollywood did to the book as a movie just so long as I didn't help them do it. But one day I picked up the paper and it said that

Below and opposite: Marlon Brando and
"sons" run off after a portrait was taken.

Page 25: Portrait of Francis Ford Coppola
flanked by James Caan, Marlon Brando, Al
Pacino, and John Cazale.

Danny Thomas wanted to play the role of the
Godfather. That threw me into a panic. I had
always thought that Marlon Brando would be
great. So through a mutual friend, Jeff Brown,
I contacted Brando, wrote him a letter, and he
was nice enough to call me. We had a talk on the
phone. He had not read the book, but he told
me that the studio would never hire him unless
a strong director insisted on it. He was nice over
the phone but didn't sound too interested. And
that was that.

What I didn't know at this time was that
Paramount had decided not to make the movie.

The reason for this being that they had made
a movie called *The Brotherhood* — also about
the Mafia — and the movie was a critical and
financial disaster. When I saw *The Brotherhood*,
I felt that they had given the first 100 pages of
my book to a real cookie-cutter screenwriter
and told him to write a switch. Then they got
Kirk Douglas to play the lead, and to show that
he was a lovable gangster they always had him
kissing little children. Then they had his own
brother kill him on orders of the higher-ups.

When I saw the picture, I wasn't angry
because I thought Paramount hustled me. That

was OK. Working for my magazines, I'd written some cookie-cutting switches in my time. But I hated the sheer stupidity of that movie, the writing, the whole concept, the whole misunderstanding of the Mafia world. What I didn't know at the time was that the financial disaster of the film made the studio brass feel there was no money in Mafia movies. It was only when *The Godfather* became a super best seller (the 67 weeks on the *Times* best-seller list gave it this classification for the money boys) that they had to make the film.

Finally, Al Ruddy, the producer, was assigned to the film, and he came to New York, saw my agent, and said Paramount wanted me to do the script. It would be a low budget, he said, so they couldn't offer to pay me much. I turned the offer down. They found more money and a percentage and I agreed to see Al Ruddy. We met at The Plaza for lunch. He is a tall, lanky guy with a lot of easy New York charm.

He was so nice I thought it might be fun to go to California. He had to take some calls in The Plaza's Edwardian Room and he apologized gracefully. "Christ," he said, "this is like the bullshit in the movies but I really gotta take these calls."

I chatted with his wife and was charmed when she produced from her handbag a miniature live poodle who let out a yip and had the handbag zipped over his head again before the enraged maître d' spotted where the sound came from. It seemed Al and his wife took the poodle everywhere, with nobody the wiser. The poodle never let out a sound while in the handbag. At the end of the lunch I was enchanted by them and the poodle and I agreed to write the script.

Fellow novelists wondered why I wanted to make movies. I didn't like showbiz. I was a novelist; I had my novels to write.

So how come? When I was poor and working at home on my books, I made my wife a solemn promise that if I ever hit it big I'd get a studio, get out from under her feet. She hated having me home during the day. I was in the way. I rumpled up the bed. I messed up the living room. I roamed around the house cursing. I came charging and yelling out of my workroom

when the kids had a fight. In short, I was nerve-racking. To make matters worse, she could never catch me working. She claims she never saw me type. She claims that for three years all I did was fall asleep on the sofa and then just magically produced the manuscript for *The Godfather.* Anyway, a man is bound by solemn oaths. Now that I was a big success, I had to get out of my own house during working hours.

"An actor's a guy who, if you ain't talking about him, ain't listening."
— MARLON BRANDO

I tried. I rented quiet, elegant studios. I went to London. I tried the French Riviera, Puerto Rico, and Las Vegas. I hired secretaries and bought dictating machines. Nothing happened. I *needed* the kids screaming and fighting. I needed my wife interrupting my work to show me her newest curtains. I needed those trips to the supermarket. I got some of my best ideas while helping my wife load up the shopping cart. But I had made a solemn promise to get out of the house. So, OK. I'd go to Hollywood.

It's true — success really throws a writer. For a year I had wandered around having "a good time." It wasn't that great. It was OK, but it wasn't great. And then remember that for 20 years I had lived the life of a hermit. I had seen a few close personal friends on occasion for dinner. I had spent evenings with my wife's friends. I had gone to movies. I had taught my children how to gamble with percentages. But mostly I had been living in my own head, with all my dreams, all my fantasies. The world had passed me by. I didn't know how much men had changed, women had changed, girls had changed, young men had changed, how society and the very government had changed.

Also I had always been very content to be an observer at the few parties I went to over the years. I rarely initiated a conversation or a friendship. Suddenly I didn't have to. People seemed genuinely delighted to talk to me, to listen to me; they were charming to me and I loved it. I became perhaps the most easily charmed guy in the Western Hemisphere. And it helped that the people were for the most part genuinely charming people. It was easy to stop being a hermit; in fact it was a pleasure. So I had the courage to leave for Hollywood.

The deal for the script was agreeable: $500 a week expense money, nice money, up front (sure money), *plus* 2 1/2 percent of net profit. A fair deal in the marketplace of that time, especially since Al Ruddy had gotten his job by saying he could produce the picture for only a million.

But the deal was not as good as it sounded. For one thing, a suite at the Beverly Hills Hotel was $500 a week, so that wiped out the expense money right there. Plus the fact that my 2 1/2 percent was worth zero unless the picture became a big blockbuster like *Love Story.* The way it works is that the studio usually legally snatches all profits from anybody working on a percentage of net profit. They do this with bookkeeping. If the picture costs $4 million, they add another million for studio overhead. They charge advertising-department costs to pictures that make money. They have accountants who make profits disappear like Houdini.

Again, let it be clear that this is not to mean that Hollywood is less honest than publishing. The paper-back publisher called Lancer Books makes Hollywood studios look like Diogenes. Lancer Books advertised that it sold nearly 2 million copies of *The Fortunate Pilgrim.* It only paid me for approximately 30 percent of that amount.

Still OK. In America nobody blames any businessman who hustles. But then Lancer put out an original paperback called *The Godmother.* I figured that no matter what they told me about Hollywood, it could never sink that low. (Sure enough, it wasn't Hollywood. In Italy they made a film starring my idol, Vittorio De Sica, called *The Godson.*)

So I went to Hollywood absolutely sure it held no surprises for me. I was armored. *The*

Godfather was *their* picture, *not mine.* I would be cool. I would never let my feelings get hurt. I would never get proprietary or paranoid. I was an employee.

California had a lot of sunshine and a lot of fresh air and a lot of tennis courts. (I'd just discovered tennis and was crazy about it.) I'd get healthy and skinny.

The Beverly Hills Hotel is for me the best hotel in the world. It is a rambling three-story affair surrounded by gardens, its own bungalows, a swimming pool, and the famous Polo Lounge. Also a tennis court whose pro, Alex Olmeda, called me Champ. Of course, he called everybody Champ. Still …

The service is superb and friendly without being familiar. It is the only hotel I've ever been in that made me feel altogether comfortable. But it did wipe out my $500-a-week expense money and more besides.

My office was fun. I loved the Paramount lot with its fake Western town, its little alleyways, its barrack-like buildings, its general atmosphere that made me feel I was in the twilight zone. I had my place on the third floor, out of traffic, just as I liked it. Al Ruddy had his much more elaborate HQ down on the first floor and we both could just run up and down the stairs to see each other.

My office wasn't really that great but I didn't mind. I had a refrigerator and an unlimited supply of soda pop free. And I had an adjoining office for my secretary and a telephone with a buzzer and four lines. This was living.

So I spent the next two weeks playing

tennis and seeing friends of mine from New York who had settled in California. Also I had conferences with Robert Evans, the head of production for Paramount Pictures, and Peter Bart, his right-hand man.

I had read once a *Life* magazine article on Evans, a savage put-down. So I was surprised to find that he was easy and natural. I liked Evans right off for one reason. There were five of us having a conference in his office. He had to take a private phone call. So he stepped into a little closet to take it. Now Louis B. Mayer would have told the four of us to squeeze into the closet and shut the door so that we wouldn't hear him take the call at his desk.

Evans was unpretentious and usually said or seemed to say exactly what he thought. He said it the way children tell truths, with a curious innocence that made the harshest criticism or disagreement inoffensive. He was unfailingly courteous, to me at any rate. If this seems too flattering a portrait of a film-studio chief, let me add that he was so cheap about handing out his Cuban cigars that I had to sneak into his office when he wasn't around to steal some.

Evans was open to argument and he could often be swayed. He was of course charming, but everybody in the movie business is charming, in fact everybody in California is charming, except: Peter Bart, who has a cold intelligence and is the only uncharming guy in the movie business whom I met. He didn't say much either. The reason for this (though I didn't know it at the time) is because he liked to think things out before voicing an opinion, and he hadn't yet

picked up the California trick of being charming while he was thinking.

The first conference went over very well. There were Evans, Al Ruddy, Peter Bart, Jack Ballard, and myself. Ballard is a Yul Brynner-headed guy who keeps track of production costs on a movie. Self-effacing, but producers and directors shook in their boots when he totaled tabs on their costs. Evans directed the meeting. It was a general conversation with a built-in pep talk intended for me. This was going to be the big movie for Paramount. I had to come through. This picture would "SAVE" Paramount. I love that kind of stuff, it makes me feel important and I work twice as hard. (I really wanted to "SAVE" Paramount but I was too late. *Love Story* did it before me.) Then we talked casting. I suggested Marlon Brando for the role of the Godfather. They were kind to me but I got the impression my stock had dropped 50 points.

Al Ruddy suggested Robert Redford for the role of Michael, and I didn't care how nice a guy he was, his stock dropped 50 points. I spoke out and was pleasantly surprised when Evans

Below and opposite: Al Pacino playing handball between scenes.

and Bart agreed with me. It was going to be a fair fight, I thought.

They had no director. I had to write the script before they got a director. Directors like to read scripts before they sign. Well, that was what I was in California for. I assured them I was one of the best technicians of the Western world (not bragging; technique can be measured. You can't brag about art).

All this had happened at the Paramount studio's plush headquarters on Canon Drive. When Al Ruddy and I got back to his comparatively humble office on the Paramount studio lot, we were just like soldiers returning to the front lines and finally rid of the brass.

"You just do what you want to do," Ruddy said. "You're the writer. But do me a favor. Start off with a love scene between Michael and Kay." He still wanted Redford.

"Al," I said as I drank his whiskey and smoked his cigars, "you can't start *The Godfather* off with a love scene. It ain't fitting."

He recognized the tagline and he laughed. He was a New York City street guy and I felt

"Anyone of my generation who tells you he hasn't 'done Brando' is lying."

— JAMES CAAN

Above: Marlon Brando is laughing because Lenny Montana (right) has just stuck out his tongue, and on it is a piece of paper that says, "Fuck You."

Opposite: Marlon Brando is smiling because he has added heavy weights to his stretcher to make it more difficult for the bearers to carry him up the stairs.

comfortable with him. "Listen," he said, "just try it. We can always cut it out later."

"OK," I said. I went back upstairs and read the contract and, sure enough, it said the producer can tell the writer how to write the script. I had to start off the movie with a youthful love scene. So I wrote it and it was lousy. I showed it to Al and he loved it.

That made me happy. Love my work, I love you. But I still knew he was wrong. I spent the next three days playing tennis. Hell, I spent the next two weeks playing tennis. Then I decided to go home for a couple of weeks. I missed my wife and kids. And this was April and spring is a good time to be in New York.

Ruddy took the decision like a gentleman. He even kept paying me the $500-a-week expense money while I was living at home. I stayed home for a couple of weeks and did some work and then flew back to California with a stop at Las Vegas, where I lost what I had saved of my expense money.

So from April to August I led an ideal existence: California, tennis, and sunshine — until I got homesick, then home again. Then when home life got on my nerves — back to California. Nobody knew where I was or when. Meanwhile I was being charmed out of my shoes by all the people I met in California. Socially, I had round heels; there was no other word for it. I wasn't getting much work done, but nobody seemed to be worrying.

Now the fact that I was a hermit escaped from his hut after 20 years doesn't mean I was a complete innocent. But the fact is that the people in the movie world are genuinely charming even if their charm is sometimes not

disinterested. One of the greatest surprises for me was to find actresses and actors so sympathetic. Writers and directors and producers always put performers down. Star actors are considered dunderheads. Actresses are always to be manipulated by power, in their personal and professional life. They are supposed not to have intelligence or sensitivity.

I quite simply found the reverse to be often true. I found many of them intelligent, quiet, sensitive, and shy. I observed that at the beginnings of their careers and afterward they are badly exploited by their producers, studios, and agents and assorted hustlers. They suffer the most profound humiliations just to get a chance to use their art. After seeing what they go through at the beginning of their careers and considering the long years of waiting, it is easy to excuse their excesses when they become famous and powerful.

From April to August of 1970 I commuted back and forth from New York to Los Angeles, working on the script, playing tennis, getting a taste of the social life in Hollywood. All very

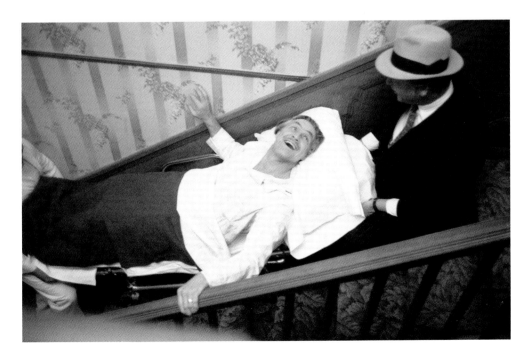

pleasant. The time before a writer delivers the script is sort of a honeymoon time. Love is everywhere.

I used to enjoy watching the pretty girls making the rounds of the producers' offices to read for parts. Every studio has a gang of producers who rent offices on the lot while getting a picture ready for production. Nine hundred and ninety-nine out of a thousand of these pictures never get made, but meanwhile the producers have people coming in to read and rehearse parts, study scripts, and have long earnest discussions on how to play the parts. Outside the studios there are another 10,000 hopefuls who have written scripts and carry three containers of film to shoot their own independent movie. They, too, are interviewing and rehearsing the 1 million pretties, young women and men in America who have flocked to L.A. to get in films. All this, combined with the great weather and sunshine, gave Hollywood an ambience that was, to me at least, interesting.

Sometimes I'd see a movie in a private screening room. No fun. People took phone

calls and messages while watching. Made jokes, talked. When I go to a movie I'm a true believer. Or I just walk out.

In the evenings I'd drop down to Al Ruddy's office and have a drink with him and his production staff. Al was an easy guy to be with, a great storyteller, and his people were agreeable. It was one of the nicest parts of the day. Ruddy was also in the middle of cutting his picture *Little Fauss and Big Halsy* starring Robert Redford and Michael Pollard, and he was always telling us what a great movie it was going to be and how many Oscars it was sure to win. Other people who had seen the rough cut agreed. I was anxious to see it and Ruddy said he would show me a piece of it first chance.

He did, the next day, a 10-minute segment, and I loved it. My New York friend George Mandel, who was on assignment from *Life* magazine to do a piece on me, disagreed. He gave his reasons, and because I think he's the smartest guy in the world, I listened. But I still liked the segment. One of the hardest things for a person to do is really to listen to the smartest guy in the world.

When *Little Fauss and Big Halsy* came out, it was a flop. Everything George Mandel had said about the 10-minute segment proved to be true about the rest of the picture. I could see it when I saw the whole thing, but it took the smartest man in the world to figure it out from just seeing a 10-minute segment.

By this time I was anxious to give Paramount a great script and make a great movie. I was becoming possessive; it was becoming my movie after all. Of course I knew my place in the batting order (eighth), but I was so psyched up, I said the first draft was just rough and didn't count, which was equivalent to giving them a free rewrite worth about 25 grand. I wanted them to love me and to show I was really rooting for our side. I didn't know that as soon as I said the first draft was free nobody would read it.

Then two things happened that made me stop embarrassing them with such sentimentality.

One evening I dropped into Ruddy's office as he was on the phone. While talking, he rewrote a script he was about to produce for another studio. I watched, fascinated. He was actually writing while talking on the phone. I've always admired people who could do two things at one time. This was special. His closing words on the phone were "I think I got this script licked now."

Now this story is not meant to enrage writers. Nor is it meant to put down producers. But it restored my perspective. I went back to playing tennis for the next five days and let the script lie. It was *not my* movie. I guess I should explain why I found this incident not annoying or threatening to me as a writer. You often read how a star rewrites his or her lines, how a director "fixes up" a script or a producer gives it a final polish. And yet if you really understand how it works, it's impossible to get angry. For example:

During World War II I was attached to the British army, and at one point we met elements of the Russian army in a northern German town. It seems this Russian division, recruited from some wild Asiatic province, had never seen plumbing. They were fascinated by water running out of a copper faucet. One fur-hatted Russian ripped the faucet off the wall and nailed it on a fence post. He was astonished when he turned on the faucet and no water came out. He assumed that water just came out of the faucet. The concept of plumbing had never been revealed to him. You can laugh at it, but it wasn't native stupidity, it was simply innocence.

When a director, or a star, or a producer picks up a pen, I think the same thing happens. (There are exceptions, of course.) They believe words come out of a pen. And again it's not stupidity. Simply innocence. They have no concept of how writing really works. So writers shouldn't get mad. They should just get the hell out of the movie business.

The second thing that threw me off involved Peter Bart. I had rented a house at Malibu for one of the summer months and brought my family out from New York. I was now seriously at work after goofing off for some four months. I had a secretary typing and I was zeroed in on the script — really in the groove. But I was past my deadline for the first draft. (If I hadn't given them a free first draft to show that I loved them, everything would have been OK.) But Bart knew I had been goofing off and started putting pressure on. I said OK, the end of the week. Naturally I wasn't ready at the end of the week. He insisted. There was still a final section that I wanted to rewrite and give it that extra polish and editing a solid piece of work needs. And then it wasn't finally so much that Bart or anybody else got tough; they were always courteous; it was just that all of a sudden I said to myself, "What the hell do I care? It's not *my* movie."

So I told my secretary to just type out the parts of the script I had already written. I didn't go over the last section. I then put on my bathing suit, and for the first time since I had moved into the house on the beautiful beach of Malibu, I took a dip in the ocean. I would enjoy a beautiful, luxurious swim.

Now this was very wrong of me and I knew it. Instead of getting my feelings hurt, I should

have just let them wait. Guilty conscience. I should have been more adult. It was also very wrong of me because I hate going into the ocean.

They had the script and everybody liked it. Of course, by contract, I had to do a revision. Now they had to get a director. This was in August 1970. Meanwhile, in the following months while they looked for a director, I had a few adventures. The most interesting was with Frank Sinatra, rated as one of the 10 most famous people in the world, a guy who had been my idol from afar. Despite this I had never wanted to meet him or be introduced. I just believed he was a great artist (singing, not acting) and that he had lived a life of great courage. I admired his sense of family responsibility, especially since he was a Northern Italian, which to a Southern Italian is as alien as being an Englishman.

In *The Godfather* the singer named Johnny Fontane has been assumed by many people to be based on Frank Sinatra. Before the book came out, my publisher got a letter from Sinatra's lawyers demanding to see the manuscript. In polite language we refused. However, the movie was another story. In the initial conferences with Paramount's legal staff they showed concern about this until I reassured them the part was very minor in the film. Which it turned out to be.

Now the thing was, in my book, that I had written the Fontane character with complete sympathy for the man and his lifestyle and his hang-ups. I thought I had caught the innocence of great showbiz people, their despair at the corruption their kind of life forces on them and the people around them. I thought I had caught the inner innocence of the character. But I could also see that if Sinatra thought the character was himself, he might not like it — the book — or me.

But of course some people wanted to bring us together. At Elaine's in New York one night Sinatra was at the bar and I was at a table. Elaine asked if I would object to meeting Sinatra. I said it was OK with me if it was OK with him. It was not OK with Sinatra. And that was perfectly OK with me. I didn't give it another thought.

A year later I was working on the script in Hollywood. I rarely went out in the evening but this night I was invited to my producer's friend's birthday party at Chasen's. A party for 12 given by a famous millionaire. Just an agreeable dinner. Everybody had been so charming to me the past six months I had gotten over some of my backwardness. So I went.

> "The kid who is ugly, sick, miserable, or schlumpy sits around heartbroken and thinks. He's like an oyster growing this pearl of feelings which becomes the basis of an art." — FRANCIS FORD COPPOLA

The millionaire turned out to be one of those elderly men trying to be youthful. He wore red slacks and a miniature Stetson and had that five-martini affability I dread more than anything else in the world. As we were having a drink at the bar, he said Sinatra was having dinner at another table and would I like to meet him. I said no. The millionaire had a right-hand man who tried to insist. I said no again. We finally went to dinner.

During the dinner there was a tableau of John Wayne and Frank Sinatra meeting in the space equidistant between their two tables to salute each other. They both looked absolutely great, better than on the screen, 20 years younger than they really were. And both beautifully dressed, Sinatra especially. It was really great to see. They were beribboned kings meeting on the Field of the Cloth of Gold; Chasen's is regally formal.

The food brought me back to reality. It was lousy. Christ, I'd eaten better in one-arm Italian joints all over New York. This was the famous Chasen's? Well, OK, the fancy French restaurants in New York had been a disappointment too. I was glad when we were finished and I

started to leave. But on the way out the millionaire took me by the hand and started leading me toward a table. His right-hand man took me by the other hand. "You gotta meet Frank," the millionaire said. "He's a good friend of mine."

We were almost to the table. I still could have wrenched loose and walked away, but it would have been an obvious snub. It was easier, physically and psychologically, to be led the few remaining steps. The millionaire made the introduction. Sinatra never looked up from his plate.

"I'd like you to meet my good friend, Mario Puzo," said the millionaire.

"I don't think so," Sinatra said.

Which sent me on my way. But the poor millionaire didn't get the message. He started over again.

"I don't want to meet him," Sinatra said.

Meanwhile I was trying to get past the right-hand man and get the hell out of there. So I heard the millionaire stuttering his apologies, not to me, but to Sinatra. The millionaire was actually in tears. "Frank, I'm sorry, God, Frank, I didn't know, Frank, I'm sorry — "

But Sinatra cut him short and his voice was now the voice I had heard while making love as a kid, soft and velvety. He was consoling the shattered millionaire. "It's *not* your *fault*," Sinatra said.

I always run away from an argument and I have rarely in my life been disgusted by anything human beings do, but after that I said to Sinatra, "Listen, it wasn't my idea."

And then the most astounding thing happened. He completely misunderstood. He thought I was apologizing for the character of Johnny Fontane in my book.

He said, and his voice was almost kind, "Who told you to put that in the book, your publisher?"

I was completely dumbfounded. I don't let publishers put commas in my books. That's the only thing I have character about. Finally I said, "I mean about being introduced to you."

Time has mercifully dimmed the humiliation of what followed. Sinatra started to shout abuse. I remember that, contrary to his reputation, he did not use foul language at

all. The worst thing he called me was a pimp, which rather flattered me since I've never been able to get girlfriends to squeeze blackheads out of my back much less hustle for me. I do remember his saying that if it wasn't that I was so much older than he, he would beat hell out of me. I was a kid when he was singing at the Paramount, but OK, he looked 20 years younger. But what hurt was that here he was, a Northern Italian, threatening me, a Southern Italian, with physical violence. This was roughly equivalent to Einstein pulling a knife on Al Capone. It just wasn't done. Northern Italians never mess with Southern Italians except to get them put in jail or deported to some desert island.

Sinatra kept up his abuse and I kept staring at him. He kept staring down at his plate. Yelling. He never looked up. Finally I walked away and out of the restaurant. My humiliation must have showed on my face because he yelled after me, "Choke. Go ahead and choke." The voice frenzied, high-pitched.

Different versions of this incident appeared in papers and on TV depending on who was doing the planting. It was at this time I realized how important a public-relations apparatus is. Sinatra has a guy named Jim Mahoney and he must be good because every story version made Sinatra a hero. Which made me think. Was everything I had admired about Sinatra a creation of Mahoney?

It must be pointed out that this incident was not Sinatra's fault. He was eating dinner, minding his own business. The fault is partly mine. I could have pulled away and I wonder to this day why I did not. But the humiliation did me a lot of good. I was really beginning to think I was important. Also now I have an accepted excuse for not going to parties. Before that it was always hard to explain why. Now all I have to do is tell the Sinatra story and I'm excused. Everybody understands.

Incidents like this send the writer scurrying back to his workroom for safety. Make no mistake, writers become writers to avoid the

39

Page 38: Coppola with his parents, Italia and composer Carmine.

Page 39: Coppola having a little discussion with his father, Carmine, who composed and supervised the music on the film.

Opposite: In this deleted scene Michael and Kay discuss marriage and their future plans away from the Corleone family.

pains and humiliations of the real world and real people. I started rewriting the script, playing tennis, and reading quietly at night in my suite. If I was going to be a hermit, the Beverly Hills Hotel was a great hut.

I felt depressed too, because I thought Sinatra hated the book and believed that I had attacked him personally in the character of Johnny Fontane. But a few weeks later when Francis Coppola was named as director of the film, he too had an incident with Sinatra. They ran into each other in an L.A. club one night, and Sinatra put his arms around Coppola's shoulders and said, "Francis, I'd play the Godfather for you. I wouldn't do it for those guys at Paramount, but I'd do it for you."

That story cured my depression, but Sinatra was still a presence in the making of the film. Some well-known singers turned down the part, one of them remarking he wouldn't touch it with a 10-foot pole. Al Martino wanted the part, but for some reason it was first offered to Vic Damone. Damone accepted and then turned it down. Presumably out of loyalty to Sinatra and the Italian-American League. But later Vic Damone admitted this was an excuse invented by the great Mahoney. He really turned it down because it was a small paycheck. Finally Al Martino got the part and, I thought, did it exactly right.

Another Sinatra-Coppola story was supposedly Sinatra calling up Coppola on the phone and Coppola just listening and then Coppola saying thoughtfully, "I never did like that line about him calling her a tramp." This referred to a line in the book where Johnny Fontane cursed

his second wife out. It was never in any version of the scripts even before the call.

Some very famous directors turned *The Godfather* down because it offended their social consciences, because "it glorified the Mafia and criminals." When Costa-Gavras, the director of *Z*, was approached, he said he would love to do it because it was an indictment of American capitalism. But he declined because it was too American and he felt that he, as a foreigner, couldn't handle the nuances.

Fair enough. I liked Costa-Gavras's reaction. And I understood the others too. My first novel was called degenerate and dirty, though others praised it as art. By now the only opinion about my work I worried about was my own. And I was a tougher critic than most, so my feelings were rarely hurt. What I didn't know was that there was some argument about making the movie as a cheapie and cashing in on the book's sales record.

Finally they decided to go all the way. Bart had written a critique of my first-draft screenplay that made a lot of sense, and also made up for his lack of California charm. In fact I found that I could most of the time get straight answers when I asked him questions. Which is not as comforting as charm, of course, but more useful. It was Bart who came up with the idea of using Francis Coppola as the director. Mainly because he was Italian and young. Stanley Jaffe, the president of Paramount Pictures, Bob Evans, and Ruddy agreed. Again my cynical mind makes me wonder if they picked Coppola because he was a kid in his early 30s and had just directed two financial failures, and so could be controlled. At the time they were hoping to do *The Godfather* for between $1 million and $2 million. (The picture finally cost over $6 million.)

When Al Ruddy told me the news, I had not yet met Coppola, but I knew him by reputation. He was considered a highly skilled screenwriter and later in the year was to win an Oscar for collaborating on the screenplay of *Patton*. (He and his collaborator never met.)

"The one thing Francis and I want you to understand," Ruddy told me, "is that there is no intention of his rewriting your script. Francis just wants to direct and everybody is happy with your work."

I knew *immediately* that I had a writing partner.

Sure enough. He rewrote one half and I rewrote the second half. Then we traded and rewrote each other. I suggested we work together. Francis looked me right in the eye and said no. That's when I knew he was really a director.

I liked him. And he earned his half of the screen credit. And I was glad to see him get it. I could blame all the lousy dialogue lines on him and some of the lousy scenes. He was never abrasive; we got along fine; and finally there was a shooting script.

The fun was over. Now everybody got into the act. Stars, agents, studio heads and vice presidents, the producer, the associate producer, songwriters, and assorted hustlers. Now I knew it wasn't *my* movie.

The big question: Who was to play the Godfather? I remembered what Brando had told me before so I had a little talk with Francis Coppola one afternoon. He listened and said he liked the idea. I warned him that *everybody* hated the idea. Some were afraid Brando would make trouble, that he was weak at the box office, and a million other reasons. I figured this director, with two losers behind him, couldn't put on the necessary muscle.

Francis Coppola is heavyset, jolly, and is usually happy-go-lucky. What I didn't know was that he could be tough about his work. Anyway he fought and got Brando. And, incidentally,

"You have a little bit of feeling for everyone you play." — ROBERT DUVALL

Above: Francis Ford Coppola and his protégé George Lucas visit the Lake Tahoe location.

Opposite: This deleted scene showed the hand-over of power from Don Vito to Michael, but it was replaced by a more powerful scene written by Robert Towne.

Page 44: Portrait of Robert De Niro.

Brando never gave any trouble. So much for his reputation.

The casting began. Actors would come in and talk to Coppola and exert all their art and skills to make him remember them. I sat in on some interviews. Coppola was cool and courteous to these people, but for me it was simply too painful. I quit. I couldn't watch them anymore. They were so vulnerable, so open, so naked in their hope for lightning to strike. It was at this time that I realized that actors and actresses should be forgiven all the outrageousness and tyrannies of their stardoms. Not to say you have to put up with it, just forgive it. But the one incident that made me check out of the casting stuff was when a quite ordinary nice-looking girl came into the office and chatted with everybody and announced she was trying to get a part. I asked her which part. She said, "Apollonia."

The part of Apollonia is a young Sicilian girl who is described in the book as quite beautiful. I asked this nice girl why she thought she wanted the part. She answered, "Because I look just like Apollonia." This is when it started to dawn on me that all actors and actresses are crazy.

To prove the point. I got a call from Sue Mengers, who I didn't know was a famous agent. She wanted to have lunch. I asked why. She said she represented Rod Steiger and he wanted a part in *The Godfather.* I told her as the writer I had no power, she should talk to the producer and director. No, she wanted to talk to me. I said OK, I couldn't make lunch but why not over the phone. OK, she said, Rod Steiger wanted to play Michael. I started to laugh. She got mad and said she was just stating her client's wish. I apologized.

Steiger is a fine actor, but, Jesus Christ, there is no way he can look under 40. And the part of Michael has to look no more than 25.

Finally everything moved to New York. Coppola started shooting screen tests. Now the big problem was to find someone to play Michael Corleone, really the most important part in the film. At one time Jimmy Caan seemed to have the role. He tested well. But he tested well for Sonny, the other Godfather son, and he tested well for Hagen. Hell, he could have played all three of them. Suddenly it looked like he wouldn't get any of them.

Robert Duvall tested for Hagen and he was perfect. Another actor was perfect for Sonny. That left Jimmy Caan for Michael but nobody was quite satisfied. Finally the name of Al Pacino came up. He had scored a smashing success in a New York play but nobody had seen him on film. Coppola got hold of a screen test Pacino had done for some Italian movie and showed it. I loved him. I gave Francis a letter saying that above all Pacino had to be in the film. He could use it at his discretion.

> ## "One of the things about acting is it allows you to live other people's lives without having to pay the price."
> — ROBERT DE NIRO

But there were objections. Pacino was too short, too Italian-looking. He was supposed to be the American in the family. He had to look a little classy, a little Ivy League. Coppola kept saying a good actor is a good actor.

Pacino tested. The cameras were running. He didn't know his lines. He threw in his own words. He didn't understand the character at all. He was terrible. Jimmy Caan had done it 10 times better. After the scene was over I went up to Coppola and I said: "Give me my letter back."

"What letter?"

"The one I gave you saying I wanted Pacino." Coppola shook his head. "Wait a while." Then he said, "The self-destructive bastard. He didn't even know his lines."

They tested Pacino all day. They coached him, they rehearsed him, they turned him inside out. They had it all on film. After a month of testing they had everybody on film. It was time to show it all in the Paramount screening room in the Gulf and Western Building.

Up to this time I had toyed with the idea of being a film mogul. Sitting in a screening room disabused me of the idea and gave me some real respect for the people in the business. Evans, Ruddy, Coppola, and others sat in the screening room day after day, hour after hour. I took it for a few sessions and that finished me off.

Anyway, what goes on in the screening room is instructive. I had been amazed at how well the scenes played live, but they were not so effective on camera. There were tests of the girls who had tried for the part of Kay, the young girl role. There was one girl who wasn't

right for the part but jumped off the screen at you. Everybody commented on her and Evans said, "We should do something with her — but I guess we never will." The poor girl never knew how close she came to fame and fortune. Nobody had the time for her just then. Hell, I did, but I wasn't a mogul.

Some of the tests were terrible. Some of the scenes were terrible. Some were astonishingly good. One scene Francis had used was a courtship scene between Kay and Michael. Francis had written it so that at one point Michael would kiss Kay's hand. I objected violently and Francis took it out. But in the tests every actor who tested kissed Kay's hand or nibbled on her fingers. Francis called out teasingly, "Mario, I didn't tell them to do that. How come they all kiss her hand?"

I knew he was kidding but it really irritated me. "Because they're actors, not gangsters," I said.

The irritation was not casual. I'd felt that Coppola in his rewrite had softened the characters.

On screen Pacino still didn't strike anybody — excepting Coppola — as right for the part of Michael. Coppola kept arguing. Finally Evans said, "Francis, I must say you're alone in this." Which I thought was the nicest "no" I'd ever heard. We would have to keep hunting for a Michael.

More tests were made of other people. No Michael. There was even talk of postponing the picture. Coppola kept insisting Pacino was the right man for the part. But it seemed to be a dead issue. One morning at a meeting with

> ## "It's easy to fool the eye but it's hard to fool the heart."
> — AL PACINO

Evans and Charles Bluhdorn I said I thought Jimmy Caan could do it. Bluhdorn, head of Gulf and Western, which owned Paramount Pictures, thought Charlie Bronson could do it. Nobody paid any attention to him. Stanley Jaffe got so pissed off watching the tests of unknowns in the screening room that when asked his opinion, he jumped up and said, "You guys really wanta know? I think you got the worst bunch of lampshades I've ever seen." For days he had been patiently and quietly viewing stuff he hated without saying a word. So everybody understood.

All this astounded me. Nothing I had ever read about Hollywood had prepared me for this. Jesus, talk about democracy. Nobody was cramming anybody down anybody's throat. I was beginning to feel it was my movie as much as anybody's.

I had to go away for a week. When I came back, Al Pacino had the part of Michael, Jimmy Caan had the part of Sonny. The guy who had the part of Sonny was out. John Ryan, who tested better than anybody for the important role of Carlo Rizzi, was out. Even though he supposedly had been told he had the role. Ryan was so stunning in his tests of the part that I did something I had never done: I sought him out to tell him how great he played the part. He was replaced by a guy named Russo who had some sort of radio showbiz background in Las Vegas. I never found out what happened. I would guess Coppola and the Paramount brass horse-traded. I never got in on the horse trading. For some reason I had never thought of that solution.

Though the script was done, I was still on the payroll as consultant for $500 a week. Now the Italian-American League began to make noises. Ruddy asked me if I would sit down with the league to iron things out. I told him I would not. He decided he would and he did. He promised them to take out all references to the Mafia in the script and to preserve the Italian honor. The league pledged its cooperation in the making of the film. The *New York Times* put the story on page 1 and the next day even had an indignant editorial on it. A lot of people were outraged as hell. I must say Ruddy proved himself a shrewd bargainer because the word *Mafia* was never in the script in the first place.

At about this time I quit the picture as consultant, not because of any of this, but simply because I felt I was in the way. Also, in most of the arguments I had lately been siding with management, rather than the creative end. Which made me very nervous.

The shooting of a motion picture is the most boring work in the world. I watched two days' shooting; it was guys running out of houses and into cars that screeched away. So I gave up. The picture went comparatively smoothly and I lost track of it. It was not my movie.

Six months later the picture was in the can, except for the Sicilian sequences, which were to be shot last.

I started getting calls again. Evans wanted to know if the Sicilian sequences were really necessary. I could tell he wanted me to say no. I said yes. Peter Bart called me and asked if the Sicilian sequences were really necessary. I said yes. I

Page 47: Portrait of Al Pacino and Robert De Niro. Although they play father and son in the film, they never meet on-screen.

Below: Al Pacino (right) plays chess during a break in filming *The Godfather: Part III.*

then called up Coppola. He agreed with me. The money people thought the Sicilian sequences not necessary because why spend the money when it might easily be cut from the film?

It is to Evans's and Bart's and Jaffe's credit that they went along and shot the Sicilian sequences. They did listen to the creative point of view when they didn't really have to, when pressures were probably put on them to save money. And the Sicilian sequences really make the film, I think.

So they shot the Sicilian stuff and now the movie was ready to be cut and edited. Think of

miles of film as a big chunk of marble and the director cutting a form out of it. Then when he's through, the producer and studio head starts carving his statue out of it; then the producer and his editors.

The cutting of the film had always struck me as primarily a writing job. It is very much like the final draft of a piece of writing. So I really wanted to be in on the cutting.

I saw two rough cuts of the movie and said what I had to say. Again everybody was courteous and cooperative. My movie agent, Robby Lantz, said I was treated as well as any new writer had been in Hollywood. So then, why was I still dissatisfied? Quite simply because it wasn't my movie. I was not the boss. But then really it wasn't anybody's movie. Nobody had really gotten their way with the picture.

From what I've seen it's an effective movie, and should make money, maybe even too much for those Einstein accountants to hide, and so they'll have to pay my percentage. But I never did see the final cut so I can't really plug it.

I had wanted to bring some friends to see the cut and Al Ruddy said, "No, not yet." I asked Peter Bart and he said, "No, not yet." I asked Bob Evans and he said yes, if the picture wasn't being pulled apart for scoring and dubbing and never mind how legitimate that excuse is. It was the second-best-nicest "no" I'd heard. The whole business was that they didn't want strangers to see it. Or maybe because I was opposed to the ending they used. I wanted an additional 30 seconds of Kay lighting the candles in church to save Michael's soul, but I was alone on this. So I said the hell with it, if my friends couldn't see it with me, I didn't want to see it. Again kid stuff. Just because I still found it hard to accept one basic fact. It was not *my* movie.

I wish like hell the script was half as good as the acting, even though half of it is mine.

The critics may clobber the film, but I don't see how they can knock the acting in it. Brando is very fine. So is Robert Duvall. And so is Richard Castellano. In fact all three, I think, have a shot at the Academy Award. And they are good. But the great bonus was Al Pacino.

As Michael, Al Pacino was everything I wanted that character to be on the screen. I couldn't believe it. It was, in my eyes, a perfect performance, a work of art. I was so happy I ran around admitting I was wrong. I ate crow like it was my favorite Chinese dish. Until Al Ruddy took me aside and gave me some kindly advice. "Listen," he said, "if you don't go around telling everybody how wrong you were nobody will know. How the hell do you expect to be a producer?"

While all this was going on, interviews and stories would appear in various publications.

Always causing trouble. Ruddy gave an interview to a New Jersey newspaper, one section of which sounded like a savage put-down of me personally. Francis Coppola gave an interview to *New York* magazine that put both me and my book down. None of this bothered me because I'd been in the business and I knew that magazines and newspapers sort of twist things around to make a good story. I really didn't care, and a good thing too. Because I got nailed for a phone interview, and when it came out it sounded like I was putting Ruddy and Coppola down and I hadn't meant to at all. And when word got out that I was putting this collection together, *Variety* ran a story that I was writing the piece as a hatchet job because I was not too happy with Paramount. Which was not true. (True, it's not Mahoney puff.) Anyway I never read this stuff unless it's sent to me. But all these news items invariably disturbed some of the wheels at Paramount.

The truth is that if a novelist goes out to Hollywood to work on his book, he has to accept the fact that it is not his movie. That's simply the way it is. And the truth is that if I had been bossing the making of the movie, I would have wrecked it. Directing a movie is an art or a craft. Acting is an art or a craft. All special to themselves requiring talent and experience.

And though it's easy to make fun of studio brass, those who study miles and miles of film, year after year, have to know something.

One interview I have to admit depressed me. Francis Coppola explained he was directing *The Godfather* so that he could get the capital to make pictures he really wanted to make. What depressed me was that he was smart enough to do this at the age of 32 when it took me 45 years to figure out I had to write *The Godfather* so that I could do the other books I really wanted to do.

I had a good time. I didn't work too hard (scriptwriting is truly not as hard as writing a novel). My health improved because I got out in the sunshine and played tennis. It was fun. There were a few traumatic experiences but all usable in a novel and as such to be accepted and even savored.

So much has been written about Hollywood people being phony that I'm almost embarrassed to admit I did not find them so. Not any more than writers or businessmen. They are more impulsive, more outgoing; they live on their nerves, which can sometimes make them abrasive. But they gave me some wonderful moments. Once when watching a private screening of a movie at Bob Evans's house, Julie Andrews was a guest. She had just had a couple of flops and was feeling hurt. As the white screen came rolling down, she started to hiss. It was funny and touching.

Another lovely scene was Edward G. Robinson and Jimmy Durante falling into each other's arms at a Hollywood party. I don't even know if it was personal, but they did it with such joy, the joy of two great artists who recognized each other's greatness. They are both now what are called "old men," but they had more vitality, more presence still, than anyone in that room. They had both been my childhood idols, and Edward G. Robinson gave me a final treat that night.

I was talking with a young, very personable agent when Robinson joined the conversation. He, too, was impressed by the young man and finally inquired as to his way of earning a living. When the young man said he was an agent, Edward G. Robinson looked him up and down as if he were still Little Caesar and the agent a squealer. The famous face registered surprise, disgust, contempt, disbelief, and then finally

mellowed into acceptance, a kindly acknowledgment that despite all, this was still a human being. Then Robinson put his fore-finger up and said to the young man, "Love your clients. Do you hear? *Love* your clients."

A lot of funny things happened around my office while I was writing the *Godfather* script at Paramount. There were times when I was faked out of my shoes.

Most instructive was a neophyte. One day

a young girl came into my Paramount office. She was very pretty, very bright, a wholesome, charming kid of about 16. She told me her name was Mary Puzo and she had come to see if we were related. Especially since the name is spelled with only one *z*, which is truly unusual.

Well, I may have been a hermit for the last 20 years, but by this time I had four months of Hollywood under my belt. She didn't even look Italian. I said so. She whipped out her driver's license. Sure enough. Mary Puzo. I was so delighted that I called my mother in New York and put Mary Puzo on the extension. We all compared notes, what town the different parents and cousins had come from, but were disappointed to find no consanguineal connection. But the girl was so nice that I gave her an autographed copy of *The Godfather* before she left.

Two hours later I was surprised to meet her still on the lot, walking toward the gate. We stopped to chat. She volunteered that she had stopped by the casting office to put her name down. "By the way," she said, "I said I was your niece. Is that OK?"

I smiled and said "sure."

Well, what the hell, she was only 16. And she didn't know she was on the wrong track. That she should have said she was Ruddy's or Coppola's or Brando's or Evans's or Bart's niece. She didn't know I was batting eighth.

Another funny story — to me anyway. While making the movie, Bob Evans gave a newspaper interview in which he took the position that the auteur theory was not one of his stronger beliefs. In fact, that maybe pictures were more successful when directors did not have much say.

The next day Francis Coppola was mad as hell. As soon as he saw Evans, he said, "Bob, I read where you don't need directors anymore." Evans just let it pass by.

It was funny to me because by this time I didn't believe in the auteur theory either unless it was Truffaut, Hitchcock, De Sica, and guys like that. I didn't believe in the "studio chief cut"

either, never mind producers. By this time I thought the writer should have final cut. But of course I was a little prejudiced.

One strange thing. Pauline Kael writes the best movie criticism in American letters (though she does not share my enthusiasm for the work of some young, beautiful actresses). I never once heard her name mentioned in the two years I was in and out of Hollywood. I find that extraordinary. Not that I would expect them to

love her. She is a very tough critic. But she is so smart and she writes so beautifully that I'll still love her even if she murders the movie, which she probably will.

It is true that personal relationships in Hollywood are geared to the making of movies, that most friendships are functional. But within this frame of reference I found many I worked with likable and in some areas warmhearted and generous. A great deal of the personal

"Who speaks of triumph? Endurance is everything!"

— AL PACINO

selfishness I understood because you have to be selfish to get books written.

I signed to do two original screenplays, which at this writing have been completed. And I have instructed my agent that I won't do any others unless I have complete control of the movie and get half the studio. So I guess I really don't want to have all that fun. Or it's because I realize I really didn't behave as professionally as I should have on the movie.

I have resumed work on my novel. The thought of spending the next three years as a hermit is sort of scary, but in a funny way I'm happier. I feel like Merlin.

In the King Arthur story, Merlin knows that the sorceress Morgan Le Fay is going to lock him in a cave for a thousand years. And as a kid I wondered why Merlin let her do it. Sure I knew she was an enchantress, but wasn't Merlin a great magician? Well, being a magician doesn't always help and enchantments are traditionally cruel.

It sounds crazy to go back to writing a novel. Even degenerate. But much as I bitch about publishers and publishing, they know it's the writer's book, not theirs. And New York publishers may not have the charm of Hollywood movie people, but they don't demote you down to partner. The writer is the star, the director, the studio chief. It's never *my* movie but it's always *my* novel. It's all mine, and I guess that's the only thing that really counts in an enchantment.

Opposite: A dapper Francis Ford Coppola on the set of *The Godfather: Part III.*

The
Godfather
Part I

"I Believe In America"

"There are men in this world who go about demanding to
be killed. You must have noticed them . . . These are people
who wander through the world shouting, 'Kill me. Kill me.'
And there is always somebody ready to oblige them."

DON VITO CORLEONE

Page 56: Since it is his daughter's wedding day, Don Corleone cannot refuse Bonasera's request.

Below: Baker Nazorine (Vito Scotti, second right) asks Don Vito Corleone to stop Enzo (Gabriele Torrei, right) being repatriated to Italy so that he can become his son-in-law.

Opposite: Bonasera has a small but important role, establishing that Don Vito Corleone is a man who demands respect.

"Some day, and that day may never come, I'll call upon you to do a service for me. But until that day, accept this justice as a gift on my daughter's wedding day."

— DON VITO CORLEONE

"The Great Don. He takes everything personal. Like God. And you know something? Accidents don't happen to people who take accidents as a personal insult."

— MICHAEL CORLEONE

Opposite: Marlon Brando played with a cat between takes, so the cat was incorporated into the film.

Pages 62–63: Santino "Sonny" Corleone (James Caan, center) looks on as Bonasera pays his respects to his Godfather.

Becoming
The Godfather

TEXT BY SHANA ALEXANDER
EXCERPTED FROM "THE GRANDFATHER OF ALL COOL ACTORS
BECOMES THE GODFATHER" (*LIFE*, MARCH 10, 1972)

"Acting is only slipping and sliding," Marlon Brando said. The noble, astonishing head slid suddenly east to west like a Hindu temple dancer. "Just slipping and sliding," the oddly light, gentle voice repeated, and now the head glided back across wide, still shoulders. "Everyone is really acting all the time."

He said this in Rome, seven years ago, and I have been debating the matter with him off and on ever since. I am beginning to feel like Penelope waiting for Ulysses to come home; this interview is my tapestry. I weave, fate unweaves; or lawyers do, or Brando himself, who despises and forbids all interviews, though not sometimes until after he has granted them. Our original meeting was arranged, with difficulty, by mutual friends. Now we are friends, and our debate has acquired momentum and rhythm of its own.

"Are you an ectomorph?" Brando may suddenly ask. "What kind of underwear do you wear? Who would you have been in the 18th century? Did you know you have a twitch under your left eye?" I don't mind this grilling. It is part of the pattern in the tapestry. We have become yoked together, two oarsmen rowing in opposite directions in the same boat. Actor and writer, extrovert and introvert, Aries and Libra, yang and yin and you-name-it—could any two creatures be more unlike than Marlon and me? We do not understand each other at all.

I cannot conceive what it is like to be an actor. To me it is agony to stand up in front of an audience. A spotlight feels like a stake through the heart. But Brando says everybody

acts all the time. "You can't *live* and not act. If you expressed everything you thought, nobody could live with you. Say your daughter comes in wearing the ugliest dress you've ever seen—spangles here, and a big brown butterfly in the armpit. She made it in school, and she says, 'Mom, isn't it gorgeous?' Well, you can't say, 'Jesus, sweetheart, it really is horrible.' You can't do it! You've *got* to pretend."

"But Marlon," I say, "most people have

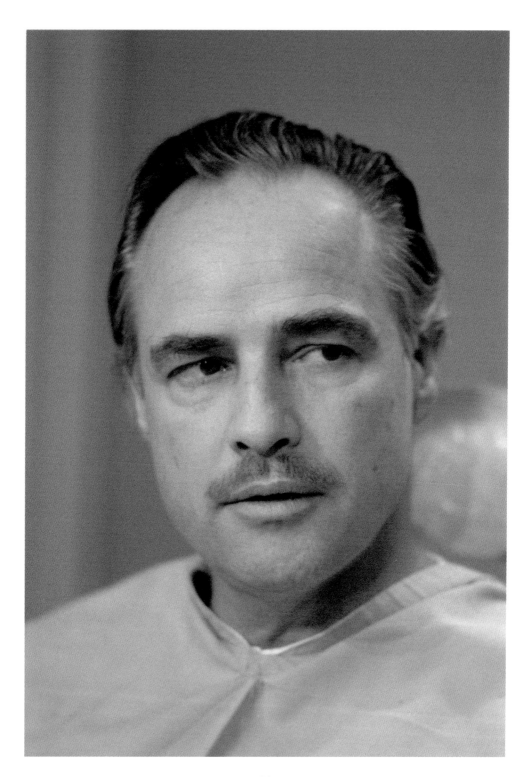

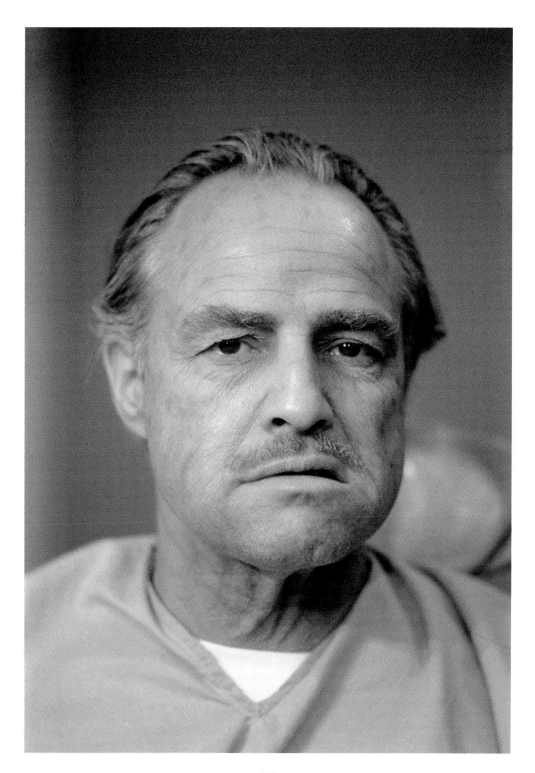

trouble not in disguising their feelings but in expressing them."

He gives me the patient-guru look. "The biggest gap is not expressing what you feel but knowing what you feel. Most people don't know."

Most people know what they feel about Marlon Brando. They think he is the greatest natural-born actor alive, and they have been saying so for a quarter of a century. I think so

"You have to upset yourself. Unless you do, you cannot act."
— MARLON BRANDO

too, but don't say it; not to him. Brando hates to hear the words. He has learned that people rarely make a declaration of love without expecting a response. They wait to hear what he intends to do about it.

When they discover he doesn't intend doing anything, they become angry, hurt, or betrayed. Success in this country has its own rules, and Brando seems to flout them all.

Our rules state that if you can, you must. Painters must paint, athletes must play, politicians must run, actors must act. There can be no equivocation. Gifts must be developed. Capacity may not be kissed off. Genius must be cultivated. Art must be served. In the aristocracy of ability, as of blood, noblesse oblige. Otherwise, life implies darkly, if talent is ignored, if the gardens are not cultivated and the paper is left blank, then everything may fall apart. Brando's heresy is that he refused to worship at the altar of himself.

Twenty-five years ago he impacted into the world of acting like a meteor, blazing. *Blazing* may not be quite the word for Stanley Kowalski, picking his nose and scratching his behind in *A Streetcar Named Desire.* But certainly it was a potent new style, not just in acting but in high-voltage sex, and suddenly the Errol Flynn and Clark Gable types became less interesting, and

the exciting new actors were Montgomery Clift, and Paul Newman, and all the other new mutations of the cool Brando style. Today we have another generation of these low-key naturalistic actors: Dustin Hoffman, Jack Nicholson, Al Pacino. So at 47, Brando finds himself not only Godfather but in a sense grandfather to a third generation of actors. Yet he is more: There is a mystery at the center of this man, an enigma that lifts him out of the chocolate box which contains every other movie star.

Do not imagine Brando is himself unbemused by the mystery, or without a moral position on the matter. He has a moral position on everything, from Bangladesh (for) to panty girdles (against). Indeed, the attaching of moral valences to every single idea, value, thing on the face of the earth may be the most predictable aspect of his fizzing, foaming mind. Caught in this constant tension, this alternating current between serving his talent and trying to ignore it, to respect it, and to exist independent of it, Brando vibrates his life away.

This vibration makes Brando far more interesting offscreen than most actors. He is also charming, fun, various, tantalizing, exasperating, tender, rude, intelligent, intuitive, kind, puppyish, catlike, leonine, slothful, and, I suppose, anything else he feels like being. He is the actor. A couple of weeks ago I went to see him in Paris, to talk to him about *The Godfather* and finish off our interview. Or did he send for me? With Brando, I have learned, nothing is fully clear. He is as comfortable in ambiguity as a sailor in a hammock.

In the soft winter twilight of the hotel suite, the figure lolling in the inevitable Japanese robe looked more handsome than ever—the head dazzling, small, perfect; a broken, noble nose; eyes that suggest bruises or smudges in a Mayan mask, until they crinkle in laughter. His longish hair is whitening and tied back with a child's ponytail elastic, leaving a becoming nimbus of wisps around the face, a sort of burning, Japanese chic. Brando glows.

I congratulate him on persuading a certain

Below: Smile for the camera, please, Mr. Brando.

Pages 72–73: Dick Smith worked with Philip Rhodes, Brando's personal makeup artist, to complete the transformation.

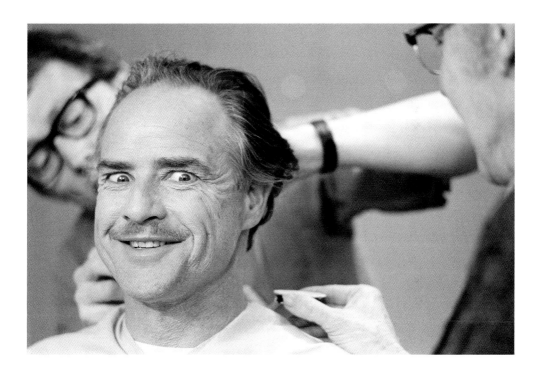

tycoon to invest in one of Marlon's many save-the-world projects, this one to extract protein from seawater. "Wasn't hard," he says. "All I had to do was rub his hump with yak butter, and suck on his earlobe a little." He grins. The dart has been perfectly placed.

On the floor by his bare feet is a copy of the *Whole Earth Catalog.* In it, he tells me, he has at last found a statement of purpose that matches his own. This and *The Godfather* are to be the only official topics of conversation. To Brando, any discussion, the merest mention in public,

of his private life is impermissible. This is why he forbids interviews. "Navel-picking" is his stock term for interviews with famous people. Interviews about one's personal life are characterized as "Navel-picking, *and smoking it!*"

"For reasons that are not completely known to me consciously, I cannot reconcile myself to sitting and blabbering to you for public benefit, and money." This strikes me as a strange remark for an actor to make, and I say so. It is why later I realize to what degree Marlon is my opposite number: To him, interviews are fake;

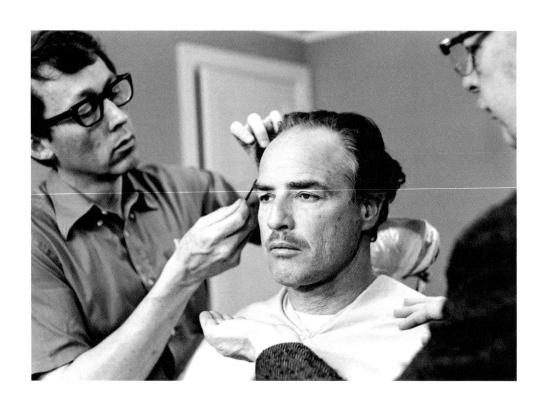

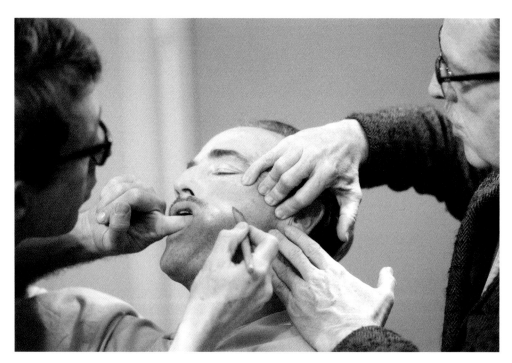

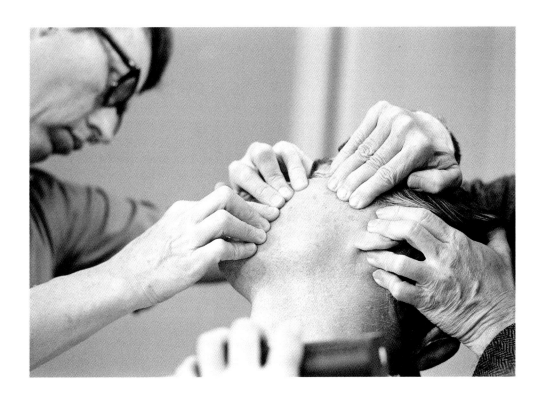

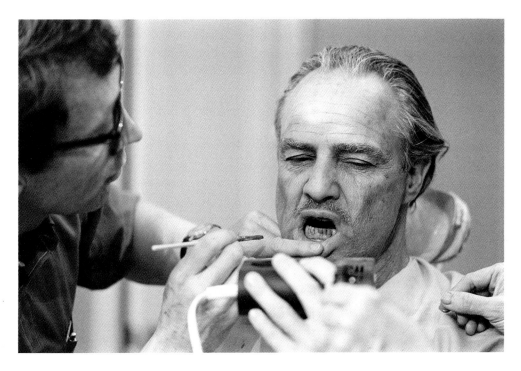

Below and opposite: During makeup
sessions, Francis Ford Coppola (right)
takes the opportunity to talk with his
actors and revise the script.

acting is real. "This reminds me of those discussions you see on television where people sit
in front of the camera and give the impression
they're having an intimate conversation," he
persists. "But it's all designed for an effect that
has hardly anything to do with the two people.
It has to do with 14 million people watching, and
ratings, and money, and other considerations
that are very carefully hidden and disguised and
painted over."

Very politely, but nonetheless aghast, he is
inquiring: *How can you do what you do?*

I try again to explain. "If I were writing about
pollution, or politics, you'd say OK. What dis-
tresses you, Marlon, is that I'm writing about
another person. And it's you."

"Look," he says, hoping once more to make
me understand. "If I were a dentist, I wouldn't
be here. If I were a lumberjack, I wouldn't be
here. If I were a scuba diver who went down with
a welding torch to fix bridges, I wouldn't be here.
But because of this nutty thing they call the
American success story, *I'm willing to be a prod-
uct!* I have my peaked cap on, and my pushcart,

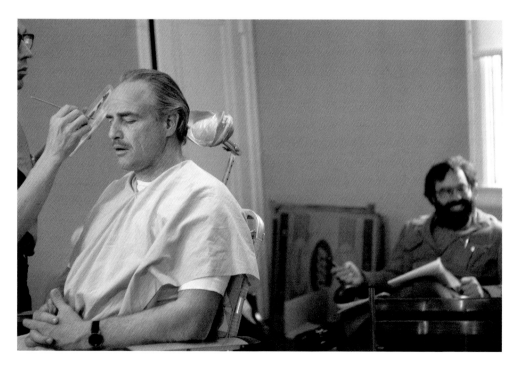

and I'm out hawking my tomatoes...aauugg-
hh...it's navel-picking, and it's odious."

For the record, then: Marlon Brando has
had a mother, a father, several siblings, and several children by several wives. He owns an archi-
pelago of uninhabited islands near Tahiti where
he spends as much time as he possibly can,
camping out with the children in a Swiss Family
Robinson idyll, a boyhood dream made real. I
remember a producer remarking once that "the
only trouble with Marlon is that his frontal lobe
isn't quite up to his lower brain." The producer
was wrong. What is unusual about Brando's
brain is that frontal lobe and lower brain are not
linked by the poor, shriveled, meandering goat
path with which most of us must make do when
we wish to visit our subconscious or commune
with long-buried emotions. Brando's goat path
is an eight-lane highway. Brando's boyhood was
middle-western, middle-class, and outwardly
unremarkable. But since this boyhood is the
deep well out of which Stanley Kowalski and
Fletcher Christian and Zapata and Napoleon

and Mark Antony and Major Penderton and
now Vito Corleone, the Godfather, have all been
drawn, perhaps he is wise not to let anyone look
into waters so rich, dark, and deep.

Brando seems able to dip into this well
at will and reel in whatever characterization
he seeks. He has been gifted with an instant
retrieval mechanism, an extraordinary ability to
fantasize, and a kind of perfect pitch. But it gets
harder every time. "It's like sustaining a 25-year
love affair," he says. "There are no new tricks.
You just have to keep finding new ways to do it,
to keep it fresh." And there are other problems.

"You have to upset yourself. Unless you do,
you cannot act. And there comes a time in one's
life when you don't want to do it anymore. You
know a scene is coming where you'll have to cry
and scream and all those things, and it's always
bothering you, always eating away at you...and
you can't just walk through it...it would be
really disrespectful not to try to do your best.

"Human behavior has always fascinated
me," he admits. "Actors have to observe, and

I enjoy that part of it. They have to know how much spit you've got in your mouth, and where the weight of your elbows is. I could sit all day in the Optimo Cigar Store telephone booth on 42nd Street and just watch the people pass by.

"But I've always tried to run acting down, tried to be very tough about it, and I don't know why... It's a perfectly reasonable way to make your living. You're not stealing money, and you're entertaining people. Everybody has had the experience of feeling miserable, of feeling: Christ, the world is coming to an end. And you go watch John Wayne ride across the prairie, and see the grass blowing and the clouds, and he grabs the girl and they ride off into the sunset. You went in there feeling awful, and you come out feeling good. *He* made you feel good. That's not bad, that's not a bad thing to do in life at all..."

What the actor does, I suggest, is to give blood to the fantasies of the audience. "That's right!" he exclaims, captivated by the phrase. "That's the great hustler's policy, one that I follow. If you want something from an audience, you give blood to their fantasies. It's the *ultimate* hustle."

Brando doesn't go to see his own movies. He feels he can learn nothing from watching himself, and might even do himself injury. "You don't learn to be effective from film, but from life. Actors who watch themselves tend to become mannered. The less you think about how effective you are, the more effective you are. If you *try*, what finally shows is the effort. Of course, this isn't true with Kabuki theater, or Laurence Olivier,

who... choreographs, and who orchestrates. But that is a different form."

He says he refuses even to watch daily rushes. It's 45 minutes he would rather spend doing something else. I say flatly that I don't believe him, don't believe he never examines his work and considers how he could make it better. After all, I think nothing of rewriting a page five times.

"Look," he says, speaking in the elliptical, Zen-master style he favors when forced to talk about something he doesn't want to, like making a movie, and maybe questioning his own performance. "Look. If I'm riding a horse, and it's supposed to get me to Duluth in 68 days from Sonora, Mexico, and the horse goes lame — I'm not gonna kick the horse in the arse. Or hate the horse. It's paid for a lot of groceries." While waiting for another horse, Marlon "would prepare myself and lay about. But when it comes time to get up and get hit with the pig bladders again — Christ! I honestly don't care."

"What are the pig bladders?"

"Well, the pig bladders are... failure."

There will be no pig bladders for *The Godfather.* The picture is as full of life as a Brueghel painting, and as full of death as a slaughterhouse. Any actor can die, actorlike, of gunshot or garrote or knife; and in *The Godfather,* dozens do. Amid this wall-to-wall blood, one is stunned by the great power of the actor who can move us by falling dead of natural causes in a vegetable garden, as Brando does.

At the beginning of his final scene, the Godfather is a frail old man, romping with his little grandson. But as the fatal seizure grips him, some of the old mafioso's bull-like size and weight magically return, and a shaggy old Minotaur crashes to earth among the tomato plants. Brando has been his own, and only, special-effects man. In dying the way we all expect to die — unexpectedly — he teaches the difference between death as titillation and death as terror.

Brando *has* seen *The Godfather*, though only because he had to redub it to banish the Brando mumble. I ask him what he thought. "I'm glad Bob Evans gave me the part," he says, "because I felt the picture made a useful commentary on corporate thinking in this country. I mean, if Cosa Nostra had been black or socialist, Corleone would have been dead or in jail. But because the Mafia patterned itself so closely on the corporation, and dealt in a hard-nosed way with money, and with politics, it prospered. The Mafia is so...*American!* To me, a key phrase in the story is that whenever they

wanted to kill somebody it was always a matter of policy. Before pulling the trigger, they told him: 'Just business. Nothing personal.' When I read that, McNamara, Johnson, and Rusk flashed before my eyes."

Brando would like to retreat to his island for good. "Being in Tahiti gives me a sense of the one-to-one ratio of things," he says. "You have the coconut in the tree, the fish in the water, and if you want something to eat, you somehow have to get it." This, he explains, is where the *Whole Earth Catalog* comes in, and he reads aloud: "We are as gods, and might as well get good at it...A realm of intimate personal power is developing — power of the individual to conduct his own education, find his own inspiration, shape his own environment." Following this credo, Marlon wants to establish a research station on his island to find ways to tap solar energy, wind energy, and the nutrients in seawater. And he is in a hurry, because "the

"Everyone is really acting all the time."
— MARLON BRANDO

three factors that concern us all are pollution, overpopulation, and aggression, and they're interlocked. If we don't solve all three problems, we can't really look to the future. Some people say it's already too late, and we're just knitting and tatting and playing Monopoly to kill time before we and the planet die. But even though you're going down in a plane, and the wing is off, you pull your seat belt tight, and say: 'Maybe I'll just make it.'"

Thinking back now over the seven years, I remember all the voices. Actors, moguls, women, yearning directors and writers, plain gossips, fans, strangers on boats and planes, and audiences around the world who have felt his mystery — all these people talking, talking about Brando. He lolls at the still center of this turning babble, not answering telephones, enraging all the talkers who can't get through to him. But what is he *doing* there? He is doing whatever it is that he at that moment wants to do: sleeping, lifting weights, making lists, dreaming about his island, stirring his fire, fiddling with his telescope, speculating about Buddhist philosophy,

tropical sex practices, bioaquanautics, Indians, Eskimos, the 10 deadliest animals in the world, famine relief, the social life of apes, poisons of the Amazon, Japanese erotica, Black Panthers …

To whoever happens to cut through to this unreachable place, Marlon will give time, money, ear, and heart without stint, and he will talk freely about all these matters, or anything else, providing it is not for publication. In fact, the one and only thing he finds difficult to talk about, even in private conversation, is acting. That is why this marathon interview has gone on for seven years. I have come to realize at last that perhaps an actor like Brando who unspools everything out of himself *dares* not discuss acting much. To do so might risk giving oneself away, mouthful by mouthful, until no one is left, no persona inside his skin. But he has been understandably reluctant all along, or too courteous perhaps, to say flat out that it appears to him that I have been suggesting that he unweave *his* tapestry so that, from its raveled threads, I may weave mine.

Opposite: Portrait of Brando, in costume, ready to begin filming.

Page 80: Don Vito Corleone at his daughter's wedding party.

"An Offer He Couldn't Refuse"

"That's my family, Kay. It's not me."

MICHAEL CORLEONE

"Life is on the wire — the rest is just waiting."

— AL PACINO

Pages 82–83: The wedding party takes place inside the Corleone compound in the late summer of 1945.

Pages 84–85: The bridesmaids (in pink) and guests enjoy the celebration.

Pages 86–87: Marlon Brando and Francis Ford Coppola choreograph the scene.

Left: Don Emilio Barzini (Richard Conte), the head of the Barzini family.

Opposite: Peter Clemenza (Richard Castellano) is the life and soul of the party. He is also a caporegime for the Corleone family.

Below: In contrast to the Corleone family, the Barzini entourage are reserved and on their guard during the wedding.

Opposite: Don Corleone and Don Emilio Barzini cautiously embrace, flanked by brothers Fredo Corleone (John Cazale) and Sonny Corleone (James Caan).

Pages 92–93: Sonny Corleone enthusiastically greets his war-hero brother, Michael Corleone (Al Pacino), who has brought his girlfriend Kay Adams (Diane Keaton).

"A friend should always underestimate your virtues and an enemy overestimate your faults."

— DON VITO CORLEONE

Below: Michael uses the wedding as a way of introducing his Italian family to his WASP girlfriend, Kay Adams.

Opposite: Al Pacino with Marlon Brando in the background.

Pages 96–97: Filming Luca Brasi's speech. Former world-champion wrestler Lenny Montana was so nervous that his speech was all mixed up, so Coppola incorporated this into his character.

Page 98: Coppola works on a scene with Robert Duvall and Marlon Brando.

Page 99: As the eldest son and underboss, Sonny is heir to the Godfather's position — he tries the seat for size.

"Francis is an emotional voyeur.
He looks, he sees, he watches
people's emotions. He can't help it."

— AL PACINO

"A Man Who Doesn't Spend Time With His Family Can Never Be A Real Man"

"I have but one heart / this heart I bring you /
I have but one heart / To share with you /
I have but one dream / That I can cling to /
You are the one dream / I pray comes true."

JOHNNY FONTANE

Page 100: World-famous singer Johnny Fontane (Al Martino) serenades the bride Connie Corleone Rizzi (Talia Shire).

Pages 102–103: Heartthrob Johnny Fontane creates a stir when he arrives.

Pages 104–105: Johnny Fontane in full flow.

Above: Johnny explains to his Godfather that he wants a role in a film that is perfect for him.

Opposite: Don Vito mocks Johnny's attitude, saying he is like a Hollywood *finocchio* [homosexual] who cries like a woman.

Below: Johnny and Don Corleone toast
one another with Mama Corleone (Morgana
King) between them.

Opposite: Johnny embraces his Godfather.

"I've almost never seen a movie that gave any real sense of what it was like to be an Italian-American. That's what those weddings were like: the decorations, the dances were all exactly as I remembered them."

— FRANCIS FORD COPPOLA

"Italians have a little joke, that the world is so hard a man must have two fathers to look after him, and that's why they have Godfathers."

— TOM HAGEN

Opposite: A quiet moment for Marlon Brando.

"Come Live Your Life With Me"

"Give him a living, but never discuss
the family business with him."

DON VITO CORLEONE

"I learned a lot of my craft from children.
Kids really turn me on — they are the most
uninhibited audience of all."

— AL PACINO

Page 112: The newlyweds: Connie Corleone Rizzi and Carlo Rizzi (Gianni Russo).

Pages 114–115: At a wedding, the children have the run of the place. Here Brando is charmed by a pair of bridesmaids.

Left: Brando was the center of attention during the shoot. Here Talia Shire gives him a neck rub.

Opposite: Behind Connie and her father is the wedding cake donated by Nazorine the baker.

Below: James Caan performs some magic.

Opposite: Jazz singer Morgana King plays Brando's wife in the film.

Pages 120–121: The family wedding photo: Tom, his wife Theresa (Tere Livrano), Fredo, Carlo, Connie, Mama Corleone, Don Vito, Sonny, his wife Sandra (Julie Gregg), Michael, Kay, and, at far right, Sonny's mistress, Lucy Mancini (Jeannie Linero).

Pages 122–123: Francis Ford Coppola directs the cast and crew.

"You've got the wrong idea of my father and the Corleone family. My father is a businessman trying to provide for his wife and children and those friends he might need someday in a time of trouble. He doesn't accept the rules of the society we live in because those rules would have condemned him to a life not suitable to a man like himself, a man of extraordinary force and character."

— MICHAEL CORLEONE

Opposite: The first dance belongs to the father.

Pages 126–127: A proud father saying good-bye to his daughter.

"What you have to understand is that he considers himself the equal of all those great men like presidents and prime ministers and Supreme Court justices and governors of the states. He refuses to accept their will over his own."

— MICHAEL CORLEONE

Opposite: Don Vito Corleone, dressed soberly for the visit to his dying friend.

Pages 130–131: In this deleted scene, Don Vito leaves the wedding with his sons to visit his dying *consigliere* [counselor], Genco Abbandando.

Pages 132–133: Don Vito with his sons Michael, Santino, and Fredo.

"The first time I almost got fired was over the casting. I think I only stayed on and finally got Pacino because literally they made a corporate decision: 'If we don't do it now, we'll delay for six months, and the book's a best seller now.' I think they decided it would be more trouble to fire me."

— FRANCIS FORD COPPOLA

Opposite: In a deleted scene, Don Vito comments on the war medals his son Michael has received for bravery: "What miracles you do for strangers."

Page 136: Luca Brasi is assassinated.

"Why Do I Deserve This . . . Generosity?"

"Sollozzo is known as 'The Turk.' He's supposed
to be very good with a knife, but only in matters
of business or some sort of reasonable complaint.
His business is narcotics."

TOM HAGEN

Pages 138–139: At the Genco Olive Oil Co., Don Vito meets Virgil "The Turk" Sollozzo (Al Lettieri, holding hat), whose business is narcotics.

Below: There is tension in the room as everybody waits for the Don's answer.

Opposite: Sonny Corleone speaks out of turn, and is reprimanded by his father. The don declines Sollozzo's business offer.

Pages 142–143: Cinematographer Gordon Willis filming the assassins.

Pages 144–145: Filming the don crossing the street to buy some oranges outside his office.

"Signor Sollozzo, my no is final, and I wish to congratulate you on your new business, and I know you'll do very well; and good luck to you — especially since your interests don't conflict with mine. Thank you." — DON VITO CORLEONE

"Never get angry.
 Never make a threat.
 Reason with people."

— *DON VITO CORLEONE*

Pages 146–147, 148: The don running for cover, dropping the oranges.

Pages 149, 150–151: The assassins shoot.

Below and opposite: Fredo is helpless to stop the attack.

Pages 154–155: Fredo's despair.

Sort Of A Home Movie

TEXT BY NICHOLAS PILEGGI
EXCERPTED FROM "THE MAKING OF
THE GODFATHER — SORT OF A HOME MOVIE"
(*THE NEW YORK TIMES*, AUGUST 15, 1971)

Page 156: Brando receives the applause of the onlookers. In the background a propman collects the oranges.

Opposite: Marlon Brando and John Cazale filming the assassination scene on Mott Street, New York.

Page 160: Coppola goes over the scene with Brando.

As was his custom before the drive home from work with his son, the old man walked across the narrow, tenement-lined street in Manhattan's Little Italy to buy some fresh fruit. The grocer, who had known him for many years, helped the old man sort out some prize oranges and, as a gift, handed him a perfectly ripened, homegrown fig. The old man smiled, accepted the backyard offering with a slight nod, and started toward his car. It was then that he spotted two gunmen.

He called out to his son and began to sprint toward the safety of his car with surprising speed for a man of his age, but the gunmen were too quick. As they opened fire, the old man seemed caught in a great leap, suspended momentarily in the air, his arms thrown protectively around his head. Loud shots hammered through the street, bright oranges rolled across the gray pavement, and the old man crashed onto the fender of his car and collapsed. The people of Mott Street watched in silence from tenement windows, fire escapes, and rooftops as the gunmen slipped away. Then, to spontaneous applause, the grim street tableau came to life, and the old man—the Godfather, Marlon Brando—lifted himself slowly from the ground, smiled at the cheering crowd, and bowed.

At 11 o'clock on April 12, just as Brando was getting shot on Mott Street, Carlo Gambino, one of New York's real godfathers, sat around the corner in a Grand Street café, sipping black coffee from a glass and holding 18th-century Sicilian court in 20th-century New York. He had arrived moments earlier in the company of his brother, Paul, and five bodyguards. It was his custom, as well as his duty as head of a Mafia family, to hear at regular intervals the endless woes of racketeers, dishonored fathers, and deportable husbands. They were ushered before him, one at a time, from a waiting area in a restaurant across the street. He was the final judge to people still willing to accept his decisions as law.

Back on Mott Street, two mafiosi assigned to observe the movie production were unaware of his arrival. For hours, they had been watching Brando getting shot. They had had innumerable cups of coffee and had adjusted their open-throat, hand-ironed shirts so often that their collars had begun to wilt. Neither of them had been impressed when they heard Brando was to play the Godfather, so they watched his performance critically. They volunteered to grips, camera-men, and extras that they would have preferred Ernest Borgnine or Anthony Quinn.

"A man of that stature," one of them said, pointing to Brando, "would never wear a hat like that. They never pinched them in the front like that. Italian block, that's the way they wore them, Italian block."

They did not like Brando's wearing his belt below his trouser loops, either.

"He makes the old man look like an iceman. That's not right. A man like that had style. He should have a diamond belt buckle. They all had diamond belt buckles. And a diamond ring and tie clasp. Those old bosses loved diamonds. They all wore them. Brando makes the guy look like an iceman."

Brando did not look like the traditional double-breasted, wide-lapelled, blue-serge racketeer. On the advice of an Italian-American friend, and not the mafiosi, he made himself look old and bent. He wore a sack-shaped suit of an undistinguished brown stripe and an outsize overcoat. He wore a cardboard-stiff white shirt with a collar at least two sizes too large and a striped tie so indifferently knotted that its back, label and all, faced front. The makeup man, who was never very far away, had fixed Brando with an elaborate mouth plate that made his jaw heavy and extended his jowls. Brando's complexion was sallow, his eyes were made to droop on the side, and with his graying temples and mustache many people on Mott Street that day did not recognize him until the filming began.

The two mafiosi did approve the vintage cars and were amused by the street lamps, pushcarts, and prices, circa 1940, tacked up in store windows.

But they did not like the way the Godfather's assassins fired their guns.

"They hold pieces like flowers," one said.

Shortly before noon a third man came up behind the pair and whispered:

"The old man's around the corner."

The two men were stunned.

"You kidding?" one asked.

"Believe me, he's around the corner."

"Kee-rist!"

"Shooo!"

Without further hesitation—and with the same pitch of excitement most neighborhood people saved for a peek at Brando—the trio left the movie set. They walked quickly toward the intersection and stopped. One of them darted his head around the corner of the building for a quick peek and shot back to his friends: "He's there. He's there. I see his car. I see Paul's guy."

Mario Puzo's best seller may have started out to be just another multimillion-dollar movie for Paramount, but it wasn't long before its producers realized that to the mafiosi themselves the making of *The Godfather* was like the filming of a home movie. Before Puzo's book, cops-and-robbers novels and films about organized crime left the mobsters cold. *The Godfather* was different. When it was published in 1969 word quickly spread across the country's most regularly tapped telephone wires about this different book on the "honored society." It was their *Forsyte Saga*. It was filled with bits of underworld gossip, and its characters could be compared to live dons, singers, movie moguls, and hit men. It depicted not only their lives, but the lives of their children, wives, enemies, and friends. It emphasized their peculiar code of honor rather than their seedy, greedy little maneuverings. It dealt with their strong sense of family and their passionate loyalties. It romanticized and exaggerated their political power, wealth, and influence in legitimate business. But most important, it humanized rather

than condemned them. The Godfather himself, for instance, was shot because he refused to deal in the dirty business of narcotics. Sonny Corleone, his impetuous heir, was killed in an ambush because he tried to save his pregnant sister from a brutal husband. Michael Corleone, the Godfather's college-educated war-hero son, assumed his father's Mafia mantle not out of greed, but from a sense of responsibility to his father, who, for all his illegal activities, was a far more honorable man than all the crooked cops, venal judges, corrupt politicians, and perverted businessmen who peppered the plot.

Though certain Italian-American politicians and organizations condemned Puzo for defaming all Italians, the author heard no such criticism from the society about which he had written. In fact, shortly after his book's publication, Puzo found that some mafiosi were anxious to meet him. They wanted to compare notes with the author of *The Godfather*. They, like other fans, refused to believe that the book was all fiction. In Las Vegas he found that a gambling debt he had run up was somehow

marked paid. When Puzo protested he was told, "It's a certain party's pleasure." On other occasions, bottles of champagne would arrive at his table unordered. Multisyllabic names were whispered in his ear by reverential headwaiters, and men with sunglasses and diamond rings waved at him across darkened restaurants.

Six weeks before the Mott Street shooting of Brando, Albert Ruddy, the film's producer, was uncertain whether he would be able to make the movie at all. Paramount had been deluged with letters describing the project as anti-Italian and threatening demonstrations, boycotts, and wildcat strikes by everyone from maintenance men to electricians. Letters had come from congressmen, as well as from dozens of New York state legislators, judges, civic leaders, and businessmen.

One of them began: "A book like *The Godfather* leaves one with the sickening feeling that a great deal of effort and labor to eliminate a false image concerning Americans of Italian descent and also an ethnic connotation to organized crime has been wasted … There are so many careers and biographies that could be made into constructive and intelligent movies, such as the life of Enrico Fermi, the great scientist; Mother Cabrini; Colonel Ceslona, a hero of the Civil War; Garibaldi, the great Italian who unified Italy; William Paca, a signer of the Declaration of Independence; Guglielmo Marconi; and many, many others."

The letter was signed by "the Grand Venerable of the Grand Council of the Grand Lodge of New York State's Sons of Italy." It also informed Paramount that the studio could expect an economic boycott of the film, petitions of protest from all Sons of Italy lodges, regional meetings to plan protests, a complaint filed with the State Human Rights Division, and demands that no governmental authorities give the production any cooperation whatever.

And as if this were not enough, there were rumors of union walkouts, work stoppages, and boycotts. Ruddy could envision costly delays. He had already run into trouble trying to negotiate with householders in Manhasset, Long Island, for a site that looked like a godfather's compound. The entire community and its bureaucrats had ganged up to sabotage his efforts.

"First, they'd complain that we would bring additional cars into the area and take up parking space," Ruddy said. "So we'd promise to bus our people to the locations. Then they'd say they didn't want buses in the

> ## "Actors have to observe, and I enjoy that part of it. They have to know how much spit you've got in your mouth, and where the weight of your elbows is."
> — MARLON BRANDO

area. Some said that if we did use their homes for the mall and the wedding the newspapers couldn't know about it. How could we guarantee that? We were ready to pay, rent, replant, repaint, replace everything in the area for them. We were ready to make all kinds of concessions, but in the end I realized that they just didn't want us. They never flat came out and said no, but it amounted to the same thing.

"For example, the Godfather's compound is surrounded by a stone wall, which we had planned to build to our own specifications out of Styrofoam. Well, one day a local official arrives and says we can't build a wall in Manhasset over 3 feet high that isn't permanent. I tried to explain that sections of the wall had to be removable for special camera angles, to say nothing of the time and expense of building and then tearing down a 12-foot stone wall to run over several people's property. Manhasset was full of that kind of stuff. I began to see the place as a swamp full of quicksand, and before I drowned I decided to start looking for another site and a little help."

Ruddy is a tall, thin, nervously enthusiastic man who sees himself as a shrewd manipulator.

At only 36, after all, he had managed to parlay
the dubious distinction of producing *Hogan's
Heroes* for television and two money-losing
films (*Little Fauss and Big Halsy*, and *Making It*)
into the job of producing Paramount's biggest
potential moneymaker. Ruddy had always been
able to talk his way through obstacles. It was his
gift of glibness that got him into the movies in
the first place. According to a brief biography
put out by Paramount, Ruddy's knowledge
and enthusiasm so impressed the Warner
Brothers president, Jack L. Warner, at a party
that Warner hired Ruddy for an executive post

on the spot. At the time of this fortuitous meeting, Ruddy was working for a construction company in Hackensack, New Jersey.

On February 25, Al Ruddy went for help. He went
in search of a godfather of his own. On that night
he was driven to the Park Sheraton Hotel for
his first meeting with Joseph Colombo Sr. and
about 1,500 delegates of the Italian-American
Civil Rights League. Colombo was not only the
boss of one of New York's five Mafia families and
thereby qualified for godfather status, but also
the founder of the League, with which he had

established himself as the dominant force in New York's Italian-American community.

In the year since he had founded his group, Colombo had drawn 50,000 people to a rally in Columbus Circle; had forced the Justice Department to order the FBI to stop using the terms *Mafia* and *Cosa Nostra* in its press releases (and had watched the governors of New York, Connecticut, Alaska, Texas, and South Dakota follow suit); had persuaded Frank Sinatra to come to New York to help him raise money at a concert in the Felt Forum; and had been named Man of the Year by *The Triboro Post*, a New York neighborhood weekly. After 48 years of hiding behind his lapels, Colombo had emerged as a formidable public figure. He posed for pictures, kissed children, signed autographs, talked to Dick Cavett and Walter Cronkite, and generally comported himself more like a political candidate than a Mafia boss.

Ruddy approached Colombo confidently that night because he had previously sat in midtown restaurants with Colombo's son, Anthony, and worked out a tentative accord.

Ruddy had agreed to delete *Mafia*, *Cosa Nostra*, and all other Italian words from the script. He had promised to allow the League to review the script and change anything it felt was damaging to the Italian-American image. And finally, he had agreed to turn over the proceeds of the film's New York premiere to the League's hospital fund.

When Ruddy arrived at the Park Sheraton and found 1,500 members of the League seated

> **"All the people who tell me nice things I tend to distrust, and the few people who are critical I take to heart and get really upset about."** — FRANCIS FORD COPPOLA

in the Grand Ballroom looking very dour, he was at first confused. Colombo's son quieted a few of the early boos by telling the delegates about the script deletions Ruddy had agreed to make. He told the crowd about the League's getting the proceeds of the premiere.

"I couldn't care less if they gave us $2 million," the elder Colombo suddenly interjected. "No one can buy the right to defame Italian-Americans."

It was Ruddy's turn then. He said the film would depict individuals and would not defame or stereotype a group. It was really a movie about a corrupt society. A movie about America today. A movie about what happens to poor immigrants faced with prejudice and discrimination. He pointed out that there were many roles in the film, and certainly not all of the bad guys were Italians.

"Look at who's playing the roles," Ruddy said, about to continue with a list of non-Italian villains in the film.

"Who is playing?" Colombo suddenly asked.

"Lots of people," Ruddy said.

"How about a good kid from Bensonhurst?" Colombo asked.

Ruddy smiled. Now he understood. During all his discussions with Anthony Colombo, casting had never been mentioned. Soon, with Colombo pointing to one delegate after another and Ruddy nodding in agreement, the crowd began to cheer as bit players and extras were chosen. At the end of the meeting, Colombo himself inserted in Ruddy's lapel a pin designating him a captain in the League.

Of course not everyone was enchanted with the Ruddy-Colombo agreement. New York State Senator John Marchi felt Colombo would gain a "psychological lift" from such an agreement and that his League would "undoubtedly get more members, because the whole presentation makes it look like the League came home with some prize." When the terms of the agreement appeared on the front pages of newspapers across the country, Charles Bluhdorn, chairman of Gulf and Western, the conglomerate of which Paramount is a part, was outraged. Bluhdorn was reported to have been so angered and embarrassed by Ruddy's arrangement with Colombo—especially when the *New York Times* published the page 1, three-column headline: "*Godfather* Film Won't Mention Mafia"—that he seriously considered firing Ruddy as the producer. However, Bob Evans, Paramount's vice president in charge of production, kept a cooler head. Anyone like Evans, who got his start in the garment center, knows better than to disregard the men in the big hats. Evans knew how much trouble Colombo and his League could make for the film. So Evans prevailed, Bluhdorn's rage was calmed, the furor in the press died down, and Ruddy stayed on.

The moment he reached that agreement with Colombo, Ruddy's troubles were over. There were no more Manhassets. Suddenly, with Colombo's imprimatur, the threats of union woes evaporated. Planned demonstrations and boycotts were called off. A location for the Godfather's mall with a garden large enough for the huge wedding sequence was found on Staten Island, and Colombo's men made a house-to-house tour of the neighborhood, smoothing ruffled Italian-American feathers. Somehow, even the protest letters from Italian-American groups stopped once it was understood that an agreement had been reached with the League. When the filming actually began, Ruddy found that with Colombo's men around, instead of being harassed by neighborhood toughs, shaken down by various unions, visited by corrupt cops, and generally treated like any other movie company in New York, the *Godfather* troupe was untouchable. The owners of old-fashioned restaurants, funeral parlors, and waterfront bars who had been reluctant to rent their facilities to Ruddy changed their minds. One Mulberry Street restaurant whose owner had sworn to his regular customers that no member of the *Godfather* cast would eat in his place had to set up special tables for the actors and crew. "They're OK," a League official told the owner. "Let 'em alone." Ruddy even managed to miss being caught in the middle of a war by finishing his location filming in New York just before Colombo was shot and gravely wounded at a League rally at Columbus Circle on June 28.

Before the shooting, Colombo's power could be felt everywhere. During the New York filming, for example, the father of one project member found himself in a hospital recuperating from a minor heart attack. On his second day there, an enormous basket of fresh fruit and flowers arrived bearing red, white, and green ribbons and a card signed by Mr. and Mrs. Joseph Colombo Sr. The patient had never met Colombo, had never even seen him, but the presence of that basket changed his hospital life. Doctors began filing into his room to look at it. Smiles materialized on the faces of nurses he had never seen before. The hospital dietitian would arrive in the morning to ask if there was anything he might particularly enjoy that day. His family's visiting hours were suddenly made flexible, and orderlies appeared with the chairs, ice, and extra glasses that had been so difficult to find before the Colombo basket arrived.

Besides enjoying the benefit of Colombo's help with community relations, the Paramount people found they had uncovered the best of all possible technical advisers. Ruddy and his

assistant, Gary Chazan, began to join Colombo associates for drinks at Jilly's and dinners at the Copa. They visited a few of the League's neighborhood offices and eventually were introduced to a couple of the men about whom their movie was being made. Soon such actors as Jimmy Caan, who plays the impetuous Sonny Corleone in the film, joined the socializing.

"They've got incredible moves," Caan said. "I watched them with each other and with their girls and wives. It's incredible how affectionate they are to each other. There's tremendous interplay. They toast each other—'centanni,' 'salute a nostra'—all of this marvelous Old World stuff from guys who were born here and don't even speak Italian.

"I noticed also that they're always touching themselves. Thumbs in the belt. Touching the jaw. Adjusting the shirt. Gripping the crotch. Shirt open. Tie loose. Super dressers. Clean. Very, very neat."

Caan, who prides himself on his mimicry, says he is really indebted to a number of these men for whatever credibility he brings to his part.

"Their moves are easy. You can watch and fake that. But their language, that's something else. They repeat certain words, like 'Where you been, where?' They have a street language all their own. It's not Italian, certainly, and it's not English. One guy, to indicate to another that someone they both knew had been killed, raised his hands in front of him, fixed his fingers like guns and pointed them to the ground. 'Baba da *boom*!' he said, and they all laughed. When we'd go to a bar or somewhere, they were always known. They didn't go where they were not known. They always bought a bottle, too. They didn't buy drinks by the glass. Always a bottle."

Caan, in fact, was seen in the company of Carmine "The Snake" Persico and other federally certified mafiosi so often and had absorbed so many of their mannerisms that undercover agents thought for a while that he was just another rising young button in the Mob.

There was an aura about the production that was unmistakable, just as there is an aura of real and imagined power around the honored society itself. A few of the actors began to think of themselves as Mafia heavies. One supporting player got so confused about who he was that he joined a carload of enforcers on a trip to Jersey to beat up scabs in a labor dispute (as it turned out, they had the wrong address and couldn't find the strikebreakers). And a few mafiosi began to think of themselves as actors, demonstrating hand gestures and facial expressions over and over for their theatrical pals.

As if assuming the style of their advisers, an extraordinary number of actors and technical people began getting into various degrees of trouble with the police. One actor was arrested for driving with a forged license while another spent a night in jail when a desk officer misread the charge against him as "switchblade" instead of "switched plates." Even the off-duty cops hired as guards on the film got into trouble with their colleagues. They had been instructed by Paramount's public-relations office to buy, beg, or wrestle cameras away from any photographers

> ## "Everyone hated Brando's first day. Bob Evans started to make inquiries to see if [Elia] Kazan were available. They figured that Kazan was the only director who could really work with Brando. Finally, after the first three weeks . . . I took control of it.
> — FRANCIS FORD COPPOLA

who might have taken pictures of Brando in his Godfather makeup. Paramount had a deal with *Life* magazine in which a cover picture of Brando in full makeup would be virtually assured if the movie company could keep other pictures of him from being published. Unfortunately for the moonlighting cops, one of the photographers they roughed up was from *The Daily News*, and within 20 minutes an inspector, two captains, and a deputy police commissioner were on the scene questioning them.

When *The Godfather* opens next spring, Paramount will not only have the distinction of being the first organization in the world to make money on the Mafia, but will also have conned mafiosi into helping them do it. Now, with the film being edited, Joe Colombo in critical condition, his lieutenants in hiding, and Al Ruddy no longer available for their calls, a few mobsters have begun to see that they have been

taken. Seated glumly in their Brooklyn cafés or slouching outside their social clubs, they realize that their movie days are over. They no longer go to Jilly's and the Copa with movie stars. There are no more private screenings at the Gulf and Western Building. Today their only contact with Hollywood and the movie they helped to make is through the business section of the trade journals, where they read that their godfather is being turned into a gold mine of by-products. Paramount is selling the rights for *Godfather* sweatshirts, spaghetti, and parlor games. There will be *Godfather* pizza and hero shops, bakeries, and lemon-ice stands. Books about the filming of *The Godfather* are being commissioned by Paramount, a television series is planned, and another film, called for now *Son of Godfather*, is being discussed.

"And when it comes out," one Colombo man active in the first film's production admitted, "it'll cost me three bucks and an hour on line to see."

Opposite: Coppola choreographs Brando's slide down the front of the car.

"Blood Is A Big Expense"

"He had long ago learned that society imposes insults that must be
borne, comforted by the knowledge that in this world there comes
a time when the most humble of men, if he keeps his eyes open,
can take his revenge on the most powerful."

MARIO PUZO, *THE GODFATHER*

"I always wanted to use the Mafia as a metaphor for America. If you look at the film, you see that it's focused that way. The first line is 'I believe in America.' I feel that America does not take care of its people. America misuses and shortchanges its people; we look to our country as our protector, and it's fooling us, it's lying to us. And I thought the reason the book was so popular was that people love to read about an organization that's really going to take care of us. When the courts fail you and the whole American system fails you, you can go to the Old Man — Don Corleone — and say, 'Look what they did to me,' and you get justice. I think there is a tremendous hunger in this country, if not in the world, for that kind of clear, benevolent authority."

— FRANCIS FORD COPPOLA

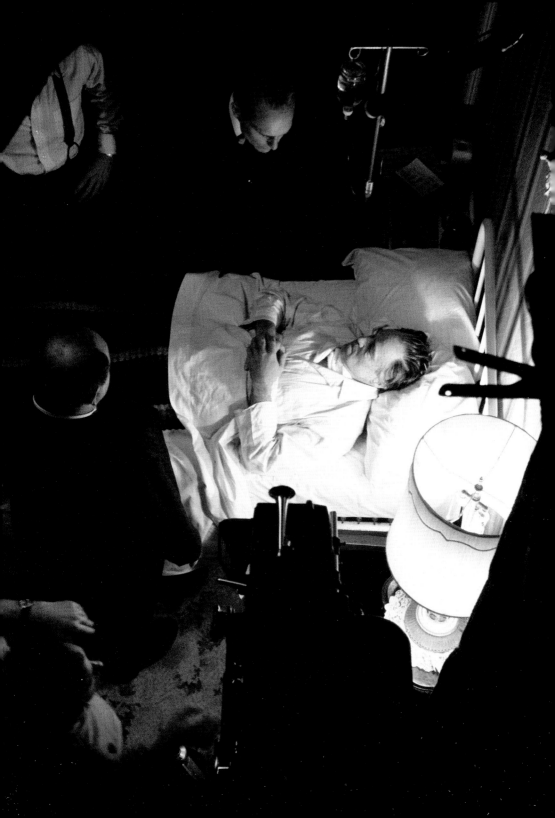

Page 168: Corrupt policeman Captain McCluskey (Sterling Hayden) is assassinated by Michael.

Pages 170–171: In revenge for the murder attempt on his father, Michael kills Sollozzo (center) and Captain McCluskey.

Page 173: Tom Hagen tells Don Corleone that it was Michael who killed Sollozzo and Captain McCluskey.

Below and opposite: The don, weak and disoriented, returns home to his family.

Pages 176–177: Hiding in Sicily, Michael falls in love with and marries Apollonia Vitelli (Simonetta Stefanelli).

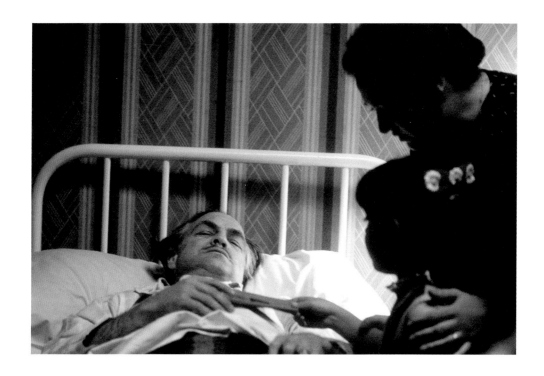

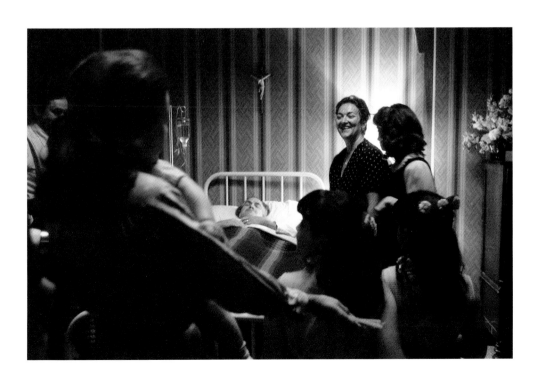

Below: The wedding night.

Opposite: In a deleted scene, when Michael
returns to America after the death of Apollonia,
he tracks down and kills the traitor Fabrizio.

"Ba fa'gul!"

("Fuck you!")

Page 180: Unlike the wedding, married life for Connie and Carlo is far from ideal.

Pages 182–183: Carlo uses the belt on Connie, and she tries to defend herself.

Pages 184–185: Francis Ford Coppola, criticized for the lack of violence in the film, and fearing that he would be replaced, increased the tension and violence of this scene.

Above: Carlo beats and rapes his pregnant wife.

Opposite: Connie calls Sonny about Carlo. Sonny, incensed by Carlo's behavior, leaves the safety of the Corleone compound to comfort his sister.

Opposite: One of the gunmen (Randy Jurgensen) who ambush Sonny at the tollbooth.

Below and pages 190–191: Sonny is riddled with bullets in his car.

Pages 192–193: Sonny dies in a hail of bullets.

"Once anybody makes up their mind to kill them there's no problem. That's the hard part, making up your mind. They'll never know what hit them."
— MICHAEL CORLEONE

Opposite: The gunman checks that Sonny is dead.

Page 196: A death at the tollbooth: retaliation for the deaths of Sollozzo and Captain McCluskey.

Making Crime Pay

TEXT BY PETER BISKIND
EXCERPTED FROM *PREMIERE*, AUGUST 1997

Twenty-five years ago, *The Godfather* was just another beach novel, Francis Ford Coppola was an arty, film-schooled director with an Italian surname, and Hollywood was a place where big-budget movies usually had singing and dancing. Here, in the voices of the people who made it happen, is the inside story of the passions, politics, and pratfalls behind a cinematic masterpiece, the only truly adult blockbuster ever made.

NOW THAT'S ITALIAN

Peter Bart: [Robert] Evans had retained the services of a terrific scout named George Wieser, who'd been a low-ranking staffer at *Publishers Weekly*. Wieser had access to a lot of books. And one of them was this 60-page project of Mario Puzo's. It struck me as the kind of picture that could be put together relatively easily. I went to Bob and said, "I know it's another Mafia book, but . . . "

Mario Puzo: Both Paramount and Universal somehow got hold of the manuscript, and were bidding for the option. I took Paramount's offer. But they didn't want to make the movie. I never heard from them again, until after the book became a best seller, and then I got the offer to write the script. I turned it down. I wasn't interested in writing for movies. [Albert] Ruddy came to town with his wife, and they took me to lunch at The Plaza. His wife had a little dog in her handbag, and for some reason that tickled me. It made the atmosphere much friendlier. So I said, "OK, I'll write the screenplay."

Gray Frederickson: We were originally gonna make it modern-day, not period, and real cheap, a million, million and a half. Capitalize on the name and get out real quick.

Bart: Charlie Bluhdorn, the head of Gulf and Western, which owned Paramount; Stanley Jaffe, head of the studio; and, I think, Frank

Yablans, head of distribution, were simply masturbating, talking to, like, 30 completely inappropriate directors, all of whom turned them down—Lewis Gilbert, Frank Schaffner, John Frankenheimer, Sidney Furie. They felt the book glamorized the Mob. Sam Peckinpah wanted to do it. I would meet with Sam and Francis on successive days. Sam could already tell you the body count— "75 of these bums mowed down in the second act" —and Francis would say, "You know, I don't really want any violence in this picture." He saw it as a family chronicle, showing how the family was a "microcosm of American capitalism." Somewhere in the middle was a good movie. It's typical of Bob Evans that when I suggested Francis he said, "I think it's a really stupid idea, let's hire him."

> "He rewrote one half and I rewrote the second half. Then we traded and rewrote each other. I suggested we work together. Francis looked me right in the eye and said no. That's when I knew he was really a director." — MARIO PUZO

Robert Evans: There was no way we could sell Francis to the front office. His last picture was *The Rain People*, which was rained on. *Finian's Rainbow* was a terrible movie. It was not a prestigious body of work. We sold it to Bluhdorn on the basis of Francis's being Italian. The reason Mafia films had never worked was because they were made by Jews, acted by Jews, and written by Jews. We told Bluhdorn, "We want to smell the spaghetti, and only an Italian can do it." Francis was the only second-generation Italian in the entire industry.

Francis Ford Coppola: I realized that they chose me because a Mafia gangster picture wasn't thought of as attractive. I was associated with the then emerging young generation of filmmakers. It was thought that I could make it cheap, which I could.

Walter Murch: Francis felt *The Godfather* was beneath his artistic temperament. In the summer of '70, we were having a barbecue in Mill Valley [California], and I remember my wife, Aggie, was reading the book, and she was so riveted, she sort of stayed off by herself reading. I remember Francis looking at that, and probably somewhere in the back of his mind he was thinking, "If it's that riveting, if it can grab somebody so much that they won't eat, then there must be something in it." He was also in a financial bind, and he couldn't turn the job down. I'm sure Francis would not have directed *The Godfather* had he not had to find a source of income.

Albert Ruddy: Francis had to meet with the Paramount executives. I sat with him in my car outside the offices and ran lines with him because I knew what they wanted to hear: Low-budget movie, don't get too fuckin' arty. We went in that meeting, he answered all the salient questions, and then he put on one of the greatest shows I've ever seen in my life. By the time the meeting was over, there was no other director they would even think about.

CASTING THE CORLEONES

Coppola: The script that had been done under Ruddy and Evans's direction by Mario Puzo had been made contemporary and set in the '70s. It even had hippies in it. I came right out and said that I thought it should be a period picture set in the '40s. My script started with the wedding party. A friend came by, and I said, "Here, I wrote this opening," and I showed it to him. He said, "You always do good openings. This is just a regular opening. Can't you come up with something interesting, like in *Patton*?" I said, "Oh well, I'll try." Then I wrote the scene between the don and Bonasera. The story of Bonasera has always seemed to me the real appeal of *The Godfather*, that you could go to someone if you

weren't being treated fairly, and the Godfather would make it right.

Puzo: When I was writing the book, and I had the Godfather speaking the don's wisdom—the very hard-boiled handling of life—half the time they were words that came out of my mother's mouth. She wielded power like the Godfather did. She could be ruthless, yet she inspired a great deal of affection.

Page 198: Even James Caan's face is wired with blood squabs, which explode when pulled.

Above: Coppola dictating notes between takes.

Opposite: Preparing James Caan for his death. Notice the wires leading out of his trouser leg.

Fred Roos: For Don Corleone, we said, "You have to have somebody who has the charisma, because he's talked about when he's offscreen, so when you see him, he better be what all this talk was about." We saw every single Italian that there was, and we realized that it's not out there among these Italian actors. Maybe the way to go is to get an incredible actor to do an actor's turn, to create a character. There were three actors who had the goods to handle that: George C. Scott, Marlon Brando, and Laurence Olivier. One day, Francis and I were talking about it, and we said, "Let's say what's really in our hearts," and we both said, "Marlon."

Coppola: Brando had to overcome the fact that he was young for the role, certainly not Italian, and at a point in his career where nobody wanted to work with him. I went to Paramount with my idea of Brando, which did not go over well at all. Jaffe said, "As president of this company, I say that you are not allowed to even discuss the option of Brando anymore." But

finally they told me that if Brando would do a screen test, if he would put up a bond so that his behavior wouldn't cost the production money, and if he'd do it for zero money, they'd consider him. And I accepted those conditions for Brando! I thought, "Well, now I'll figure out how to talk him into it."

I got Brando to allow me and some friends to go early in the morning to shoot some footage of him. I had heard that he wore earplugs because he didn't like loud noises, so I told all my guys that we had to be like ninjas. We used sign language. I went around his house and I put out little props—Italian cigars and provolone cheese. Then they woke him up, and he came out of the bedroom with this long blond hair and Japanese robe. He took his ponytail and he put it up on his head, put black shoe polish on his hands and rubbed it in his hair, and then he put some Kleenex in his mouth, and he said, "Oh, he should be like a bulldog." I was fascinated. He bent the collar of this white shirt we had brought and said, "You know those guys, the collar is

always bent." By then, of course, I was convinced that he would be wonderful. So I went to New York with the videotape, set up this old-fashioned half-inch tape recorder on Bluhdorn's conference-room table, and then I went to his door and knocked and said, "Mr. Bluhdorn, could you just come out, I want to show you something." I turned on the switch and there was this image of Brando with the blond hair getting ready to pull it up. Bluhdorn looks and says, "No! No! I don't vant a crazy guy! Absol … That's *incredible*." And once he said that, they made the deal.

Ruddy: Everyone had differing ideas of who should play Michael. Francis wanted Al Pacino. Bob [Evans] wanted bigger names—Ryan O'Neal, Warren Beatty, Robert Redford. He thought Al was too short.

James Caan: When Francis got the job, he had me, Bobby Duvall, and Al Pacino go up to San Francisco. For the price of three or four corned-beef sandwiches, we improvised some scenes on 16mm film. He sent that to Paramount, and that was his cast. So I went home. Then, of

course, all these great geniuses who take credit for everything got involved.

Coppola: The screen tests only confirmed in the producers' minds that they didn't like Al. They told me he was too scruffy—looked like a "gutter rat"—to play a college boy. So I took him into a barbershop and said, "I want to give this guy a haircut. He's gotta go back to college." Someone whispered to the barber that this was a guy who was going to play Michael Corleone in *The Godfather*, and the barber had a heart attack—literally. They carried him out to the hospital and some other guy had to finish the haircut. But when the producers saw that haircut, they said, "Oh, he looks terrible! He has no hair. He looks like a runt." So it was clear that they didn't want him, period.

Caan: Then, about a month and a half later, Paramount asked me to do *T. R. Baskin*. So I was sitting here in L.A., and I get a call from Francis one evening; he says, "Jimmy, I want you to come in and test." "Test what? Ya got a new Porsche you want me to drive around the block?" He says, "They want you to play Michael." So I go in and witness one of the great apparitions of all time. There's every friggin' actor you can imagine—with Irish accents, with Spanish accents, with Dutch accents. You name the actor, they were there. Eventually I tested for every part. I got disgusted. I said, "I'll tell you what. Stick this picture up your ass. I'm outta here." I was so angry that I got on a train and went to Chicago to that *T. R. Baskin* thing.

Coppola: Whenever there was going to be another round of tests, I would call up Pacino and say, "Please, come again." And his girlfriend, Jill Clayburgh, would rip the phone away from him and say, "What are you doing to him? You're torturing him! Don't call him anymore! They're never gonna give him the part." And I would say, "One last time, please." And he would come.

Evans: I didn't want Pacino. It's like four weeks before the picture's going to start and we don't have casting and we don't know where we're going to make the picture either. We were fighting all the time. So Francis said to me, "We got a big problem here. You want someone that looks like you and I want someone that looks like me." I wanted Alain Delon, all right? That's the way the part was written in the book. I was

> "All I remember was A. D. Flowers, the effects guy, going, 'You know, I've done I don't know how many pictures, and I've never put this many squibs on anybody before.' I was really happy to hear that." — JAMES CAAN

wrong. So Francis said, "I want Pacino, and I'm the director! You won't use him, I'm quittin' this fuckin' picture." I said, "OK, I'll use the midget."

So the next day I called Al's agent, and he said, "Bob, he's waited so long, he's signed for another picture, *The Gang That Couldn't Shoot Straight*, at MGM." I said, "This is *The Godfather!*" He went, "I'm not taking on Jim Aubrey [the head of MGM]. You want to call Aubrey, call him." I knew Jim well. But he talked to me like I had just given his daughter AIDS. He said, "Fuck you." That's where Sidney Korshak, who was my good friend and lawyer, stepped in. I called Sidney at The Carlyle and said, "Sidney, you've got to help me on something. I need an actor." He said, "What do you mean, you need an actor?" I said, "An actor for *The Godfather*." "Who is it?" "A guy named Al Pacino." He said, "Never heard of him." "Francis'll kill me if I can't get him, and Aubrey won't give him to me." "So what do you need me for? [Kirk] Kerkorian owns the company, call him." "Help me. I need it." He says, "Sit there." Twenty minutes later Aubrey called and says, "You motherfucking cocksucker. I'll get you, you no-good piece of shit. OK, you got the midget." I said to Sidney, "Whadja say?"

He told me, "Kirk said, 'I'd do anything for you, but I can't intercede in this. I've given Jim Aubrey total autonomy to run MGM for me.'" And Sidney said, "Well, Kirk, you're building an awfully big hotel there, the MGM Grand. Would you like to finish it?" Kerkorian said, "Who's the actor?" And Sidney said, "The actor's name is something like Pacino." "Spell it." "Capital *a*, little *l*, capital *p*-punk a-c-i-n-o." "Who the fuck is that?" He says, "I don't know. Bobby needs him." And that's the way we got Pacino. ["There's no truth to it," says a Kerkorian spokesperson.]

FAMILY DYSFUNCTIONS

Coppola: So, ultimately, after four months of arduous tension, I ended up with my cast, Brando and Pacino. They spent $400,000 on screen tests, which they could have saved if they'd just said yes in the first place.

Ruddy: It was one of those great moments. Everyone who did that movie needed a winner. Brando couldn't get a fucking job. Al was going nowhere. Jimmy Caan was going nowhere. No one was beating Francis's door down, and no one was lighting fucking candles to get me. Everyone got together and made magic.

Evans: I wanted to shoot it in New York. Without Sidney Korshak, it would have been shot in Kansas City. Without Korshak, we couldn't have gotten into a subway station. We go to Long Beach, Long Island, find a location, two

days later we can't get in there. Same thing in Flushing [Queens]. Same thing in Forest Hills. Same thing in Staten Island. Same thing in the Bronx. What happened was that my kid has just been born. I'm at The Sherry-Netherland and I get a call from a goombah who says, "Listen, get outta this town. You're not welcome here." I said, "Why don't you call Al Ruddy? He's the producer." He says, "If you want to kill a snake, you cut off the head. You want your kid to grow up alive?" That's when I called Korshak. Within 72 hours, every door was open.

Ruddy: When I got to New York, Bob Evans called me up, fucking hysterical. Said I gotta go meet this guy named Joe Colombo, because they're threatening him. There had already been a big rally at Madison Square Garden about six months before we got there, with Frank Sinatra and Sammy Davis, sponsored by the Italian-American League, for the sole, express purpose of stopping the film.

Gary Chazan: The meeting was in the Gulf and Western Building. They came in all dressed up for, like, a wedding—coats and ties and pinkie rings and the whole thing. They were intimidating. I said to Al [Ruddy], "Listen, make sure you don't tell these guys anything we can't back up." They really only wanted to accomplish one thing, which was that they didn't want the words *Mafia* or *Cosa Nostra* used in the picture. It was nothing but a shakedown.

Ruddy: I said, "Joe, I give you my personal guarantee that this is not the typical movie that defames Italian-Americans. It's the Jewish producer who's defamed, an Irish cop. It's an equal-opportunity motion picture. I'll let you see the screenplay." I pulled out this 155-page screenplay, which nobody was gonna read. "Here's what I'll give you, OK? I will give you a premiere for a hospital, a charity." And he said, "Look"—he turned to his guys—"do we trust this guy?" And they said, "Yeah." "So, OK, let's make the deal." So we shook hands, and that's how the whole deal was made, period. They had a huge press conference in the League's office, where suddenly I was in the elevator with 20 guys with cameras. It was on ABC, NBC, CBS, the front page of the *New York Times*, about this deal. There was an article in the *Wall Street Journal*—MOB MOVES IN ON GULF AND WESTERN. The stock plummeted. I was called to the G and W Building and told that I had wrecked the company. I was fired by Bluhdorn. He was insane. Freaking out. My comment was, "I don't own any shares in G and W. My job is to

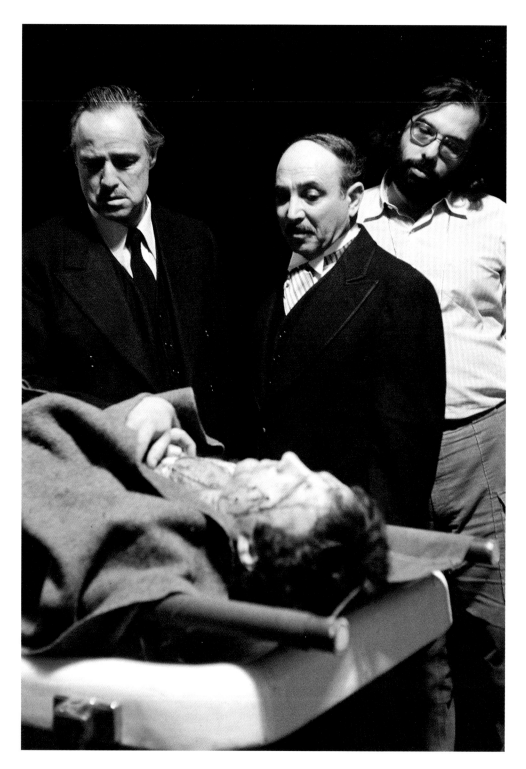

get the movie made." I went back to my hotel, I'm packing, and I'm not going to go back. Fuck him. Charlie called Francis down to his office and told him, "Al Ruddy's totally insane, blah-blah-blah." And Francis says, "Quite to the contrary. He's the only guy who can keep this movie going," and in effect saved my job. I called up the League and told Joe what had happened. He could not have been nicer. I would rather deal with some of those people than with some of the people in Hollywood.

Caan: We went up to Patsy's, an Italian restaurant uptown. Everything Francis does is very grand. So we had a big Italian feast. I'm talking, like, a huge table, 20 feet or something. The whole cast was there. We were going to have this reading. Sitting at the head of the table was Brando. Next to him was me. On the other side of him was Al, and then next to Al was Bobby Duvall. Way down at the other end of the table was Francis. So on one end you got all these Actors Studio guys—it was just mumbles. Francis was pulling his hair out, 'cause you couldn't hear a fuckin' word. It could have been in Chinese. Hysterical. Sterling Hayden, the old Hollywood actor, came in and said, "Hey! What are you guys doin'?" You heard this booming voice, and it was like the only line we'd heard up until that point.

Coppola: The whole visual style of *The Godfather* was laid out before we ever shot one foot of film. We had a meeting—myself, Gordy Willis, and Dean Tavoularis, the production designer. We talked about the contrast between good and evil, light and dark. How we'd really use darkness, how we'd start out with a black sheet of paper and paint in the light, and the camera would never move.

Gordon Willis: I discussed the structure with Francis. It was a tableau movie, meaning there weren't a lot of contemporary mechanics introduced, like helicopters and a zoom lens. The actors move in and out of frame. It would feel like a period movie, 1942. But there was no

discussion of lighting. I rarely discuss lighting with anybody. I just did it. It grew out of the juxtaposition with an outdoor wedding, this bright, cheerful thing, and the underbelly of it was this dark house where you get a sense of evil personified. We used overhead lighting because it helped to accentuate what Brando was. It put his eye sockets into the back of his head and gave it a sinister feel. You didn't want to always

> ## "I was at Paramount all day yesterday and they want me to direct this hunk of trash. I don't want to do it. I want to do art films."
> — FRANCIS FORD COPPOLA

see what he was thinking, so we didn't want to see into his eyes that much. I just kept him dark. When that stuff started to appear on the screen, it seemed a little scary to everybody who was used to looking at Doris Day movies.

Coppola: I was, like, in deep, deep trouble because the first week had gone terrible. Al twisted his ankle, and I hadn't finished the hospital scene where McCluskey punches Michael. Then the second week, we started with the Brando stuff and they hated Brando. They said they couldn't understand him.

Frederickson: When they started seeing the dailies, they became alarmed. Gordon Willis was shooting everything very dark, which threw them off. They'd see the same scene over and over again, where you couldn't see anybody, just silhouettes, and that had never been done before. Ruddy was loyal to the studio. He was staying in my apartment in New York, so I overheard all these conversations. There was an editor that Francis had brought in, Aram Avakian, who had edited Francis's movie *You're a Big Boy Now.* They started talking to him about taking over the picture. So I went to Francis, "Hey—I'm here with you every day, I

Page 206: Brando, Salvatore Corsitto (as undertaker Bonasera), and Coppola rehearsing the embalming-room scene with James Caan.

Below: Don Corleone tells Bonasera: "I want you to use all your powers, and all your skills. I don't want his mother to see him this way."

know the problems you're facing, you're doing your best, and I feel I have to let you know that this is afoot."

Coppola: On Tuesday of the third week, Gray came to me and said, "Listen, they're going to fire you this weekend," because they figured if they fired the director on the weekend, then there's time for the new guy to get up to speed. I said to Paramount, "Look, it's the first day, Brando's nervous, I'll make it up, let me shoot it again." The studio said no. That's when I realized it was true, because when they won't let you fix

something, it means they'll let another director come in. Avakian was a friend of mine, and he had asked me to get a job for his ex-producer Stephen Kesten as the AD. So now I had these two guys in there who were lobbying to get the job away from me. So on that Thursday, I fired five guys, because I was still the director. I just did a preemptive strike, and they didn't have the comfort of the weekend. I guess they must have had a meeting in which they decided, "Look, we're in with this guy," figuring if the word got out what a mess this was, it would only hurt the picture.

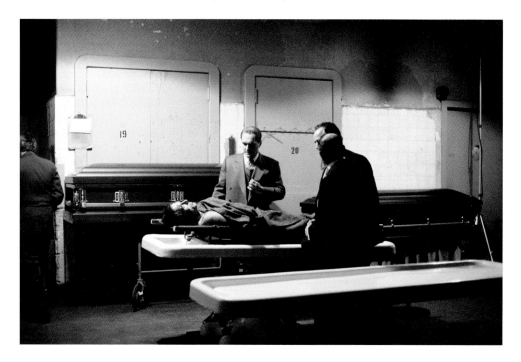

Evans: I'm out in L.A. and I get a call from Al Ruddy; Avakian; my production guy, named Jack Ballard; and the production associate on the film, Steve Kesten. Avakian was editing the scene where Pacino goes into the john, takes the gun out from behind the toilet seat, and goes out and blows Sollozzo's head off. And he says, "We can't cut it together. The guy's shooting a film and nothing will work." So I asked them to send the dailies out to me. I'm a lousy executive, I'm a lousy physical producer, but when it comes to editing, I'm pretty tight. So I edited this with one of the people on the lot. It was the most brilliant scene I'd ever seen. And I realized it was a coup. I flew to New York, gave Al Ruddy a scare, and told Jack Ballard, "One more mistake and you're fired"; and I fired Avakian.

Stephen Kesten: Blaming a dead guy [Avakian] is the cheapest shot of all. If there was any putsch, it was Paramount's. We had a screenplay that was 187 pages long, against the standard length of 120. When the second draft came in, a couple of weeks before we were due to shoot, it was 173, 174 pages, still long. Paramount was all over Francis— "We're not gonna start with a 173-page script." They're not gonna bring a writer in on Francis, because he got nominated for *Patton*. I said, "Why don't you hire Aram Avakian as an editorial consultant whose function will be to work with Francis on the script? Everybody bought in on that. Aram had cut *You're a Big Boy Now*. He had directed *End of the Road*, which *Life* magazine had called one of the most important films of the '60s.

During the shoot, the word came down from Paramount that Francis wasn't going to make it. They approached Aram. He said, "I'm not gonna talk about it until you do whatever you're gonna do." On the 15th of April, Francis got the Academy Award for *Patton*, and either on the 16th, which was a Friday, or the following Monday, he had a meeting with Charlie Bluhdorn, where he was supposed to be fired. We were down on Mulberry Street, staging the don getting shot.

We were waiting and waiting and waiting, and no Francis. Finally we get word: Francis is on his way. He came out of that meeting with his job and the name of the guy whom Paramount wanted to replace him with. He went right to Aram, and Aram was off the picture. Francis thought there was a conspiracy. I know Aram never agreed to do it. He told me that he wouldn't violate the friendship with Francis. It never got that far. Nor would he have allowed it to get that far, because he was a mensch. Aram was terribly hurt by it. He did a couple of small pictures after that, but he was no longer an up-and-comer.

MOONSTRUCK

Caan: Al Pacino was very serious. Bobby Duvall was nuts with the mooning. He was like a 12-year-old kid. The day after the reading at Patsy's, we're riding down Second Avenue and Bobby's drivin' and we see Brando in a car next to us. "Come on, Jimmy, moon him!" And I go, "Get outta here," because I didn't want to do that shit, but Bobby talked me into it. So I stuck my ass out the window, and Brando, he just fell down.

Richard Bright: They're standing at the wedding ceremony when they posed for that picture, and there are 500 extras, old ladies, old men, kids, everybody. Bobby Duvall sees the ultimate moon. He and Brando had a race to drop their pants, and Bobby's got hitched, and Brando beat him, bent over and spread his cheeks, hemorrhoids and all, and mooned everybody. And the old Italian ladies in the back went, "I didn't see what I saw, did I?" We had this belt made, MOON CHAMPION, hand-tooled leather. Brando got it.

Caan: Brando was so concentrated and available to everything around him that if a train came through the room in the middle of a fuckin' scene, he wouldn't break. There was this one scene where Duvall comes back from cutting the horse's head off; it's between him, Brando, and myself, and we're discussing something to do with Sollozzo. The dialogue was predominantly with Bobby and Marlon. There was a bowl of walnuts on the table, so while they're talking, I reached for one of the nuts, like most fuckin' idiot actors. Now I cracked it, right, and Brando looked up at me, right in the middle of the scene, his eyes kind of flashed up at me, and I could see, like, there was disgust, right? Now I had the fuckin' nut in my hand and it was right in the take, and I couldn't just put it down, and at one point, he goes, "Pay attention. That's why you're not gonna be a good don." What's going through my mind is, "Oh my God, Marlon Brando's thinking that I'm doing some scene-stealing shit with this nut." And I'm fuckin' humiliated and embarrassed, which all seemed to work for me anyway. And when it was over, he hugged me. "That's the greatest!" He thought it was brilliant. He just loved the idea that Sonny would be eating fuckin' nuts when he's discussing serious business, you know. It was great.

The scene where I'm shot by the tollbooth? I was scared to death. They sewed squibs into my suit, like 147 squibs, big time. The squibs were inch-long brass casings with a V in the middle of them, and in that V would be gunpowder, and then over the gunpowder would be a little sack of fake blood. All the Vs had to point outward, because they would blow a hole in you otherwise, which would really be fun. So I had, like, a 10-inches-in-diameter fuckin' ball of wires coming out of my leg. And then they have these boards with nails on 'em, and when you make the contact, each one goes off, *tac-tac-tac!* All

I remember was A. D. Flowers, the effects guy, going, "You know, I've done I don't know how many pictures, and I've never put this many squibs on anybody before." I was really happy to hear that.

There was a lot of unrehearsed stuff. Francis loved that. He allowed the actors a lot of freedom. I guess that may have had to do with his problems with Gordy.

LIGHTS AND ACTION

Coppola: The problems between me and Willis were sort of like the problems between someone who was trying to liberate, have the actors behave and work in a style that caught life, and the cinematographer, who wanted the marks adhered to to the nth degree. If the girl was gonna sit there, then she really had to sit there, because if she sat over there, there wouldn't be any light on her at all. He's a very mark-obsessed photographer, and actors, although they try their best to hit marks, they also are trying to give life.

Willis: Francis wasn't well schooled in that kind of moviemaking. He'd done some on-the-road, running-around kinda stuff. You can't shoot a classic movie like video theater. It's not cinema verité. You either structure it to get it right or you have a mess. You get a happy accident once in a while. But you can't shoot a whole movie hoping for happy accidents. What you get is one big, bad accident.

Fred Gallo: [At one point] Francis wanted to change the shot, and Gordy said, "Well, I have to relight." Francis said, "I want to shoot now," and Gordy says, "I'm not ready," and he walked off. Francis said, "I want somebody to operate right away."

Michael Chapman: Francis yelled, "Get me Chappie, get me Chappie!" It was a fit of bravado— "That's not going to stop me, I'll just keep on!" I ran into the john, took my pants down, and locked the door.

Gallo: Francis stormed off, and the next thing I heard, it sounded like a gunshot. I thought, "Oh my God, he shot himself." He'd kicked his door in. The unit production manager, Freddie Caruso, walked by. Freddie was a very low-key guy. Francis is red as a beet. Freddie says, "Hi, Francis. How's everything going today?"

FACING THE MUSIC

Coppola: I had a deal with the studio that allowed me to edit the movie in San Francisco, where I lived. But Evans warned me very clearly that if it was more than two hours and 15 minutes, without any discussion, he was going to yank the film to L.A. and cut it there, which I dreaded.

Evans: We screened the picture, and in there were all Francis's people—Walter Murch, Gray Frederickson, Bob Towne—and they blew smoke up his ass. We had some fight afterward. I think it may be the only time in history where the studio wanted to make the picture longer and the filmmaker wanted it shorter. He was cheating himself. He made a brilliant film, but it was on the floor. He took all the nuances out of it.

Coppola: When Evans saw the film, he said, "Where's all the stuff that makes it so great, blah-blah-blah, I'm yanking it to L.A." So it was clear they were going to take it to L.A. either

way. So we got to L.A. and we put the footage back and we said, "See? Isn't that better?" He said, "Yes, that's better."

We had a big music conflict. Evans did not like Nino Rota's music and at one point ordered me to take it out and go with source music. I believed in the Nino Rota music, so I refused. I said, "This is bullshit, you don't have the power to order me to take out the music. You have the

"If you want something from an audience, you give blood to their fantasies. It's the ultimate hustle."

— MARLON BRANDO

power to fire me and hire another director and tell that director to take out the music." Well, he didn't want to fire me, because it was late in the game. Finally I said, "Let's have a screening of the picture, invite a small, controlled audience, 30 to 40 people, and if they don't find the music a problem, we'll leave it in. If they do, we'll take it out." And he said, "Who gets to decide whether they have a problem or not?" And I said, "You can." The picture had never been shown. He'd been terrified to let anyone see it. So we had a

screening at Paramount. The audience liked the movie, the music, the acting, everything. And that was the first indication that I had that the movie would work.

Evans: We took an *R* on *The Godfather* because of me. I fought with the MPAA. There were two scenes they wanted me to take out. One was when Al Pacino is in Sicily and he marries this virginal girl and you see the nipple on her breast. I didn't mind losing that scene, but the other scene was where Jimmy Caan gets shot down at the tollbooth. They said it was too violent, and I said, "I will not take it out." Distribution was desperate for a *PG*, and they fought me on it. I took an *R*.

Ruddy: The Godfather opened on a Wednesday morning, and the fuck it rained. I was a basket case. And then I see the lines, at 8:30 in the morning! It was staggering. I had seven-and-a-half points, Francis had seven-and-a-half, Mario had two-and-a-half. Every point was worth over a million dollars. The studio owned 82.5 percent of the movie. *The Godfather* brought in the era of the blockbusters, where they're looking for the $100 million movie, the home run, the tent-pole attraction to build a schedule on. This had never happened before.

Opposite: Don Corleone grieves over the death of his eldest son, Santino.

Page 214: Don Vito Corleone calls a meeting of the Five Families to settle the dispute between the Corleones and the Tattaglias.

Pages 216, 217, 218–219: The Godfather, still recovering from his injuries, shows that he is still mentally strong, and willing to end the war, which is bad for business.

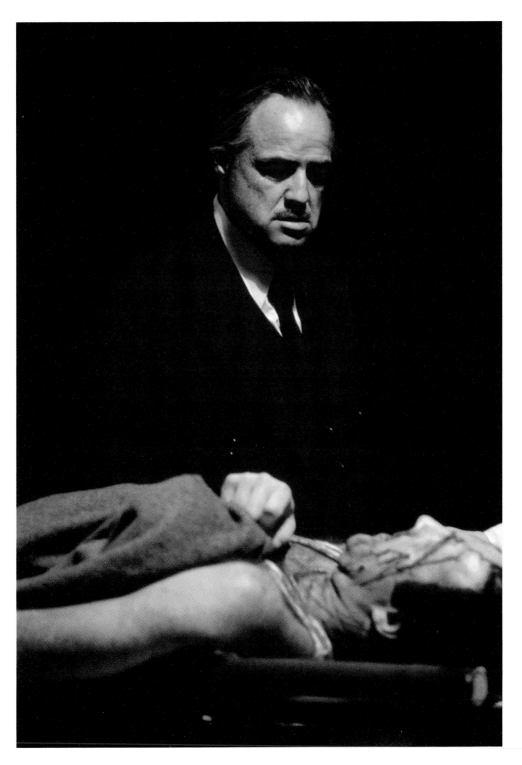

"A Reasonable Man"

"We are all men who have refused to be fools, who have refused
to be puppets dancing on a string pulled by the men on high."

DON VITO CORLEONE

"What manner of men are we then, if we do not have our reason? We are all no better than beasts in a jungle if that were the case." — DON VITO CORLEONE

Pages 220–221, below and opposite:
Coppola works with Brando on this very
subtle scene, where what is left unsaid is
more important than what is said. The other
families are looking for signs of weakness and
vulnerability in the once invulnerable Don
Vito Corleone.

Pages 224–225: Don Emilio Barzini over-
sees the cessation of hostilities between
Don Philip Tattaglia (Victor Rendina) and
Don Vito Corleone.

Page 226: The Godfather starts to show
his age.

"I give my honor, that I will never seek vengeance, I will never seek knowledge of the deeds that have been done in the past. I will leave here with a pure heart." — DON VITO CORLEONE

"Women And Children Can Be Careless, But Not Men"

"Now listen — whoever comes to you with this Barzini meeting — he's the traitor. Don't forget that."

DON VITO CORLEONE

"You see, Sicily was always invaded, and over
the centuries, the Sicilians discovered the only
way to survive the invasions was to trust only
their own families and never break that trust."

— AL PACINO

Pages 228–229: Filming the transfer-of-power scene written overnight by Robert Towne.

Pages 230–231: This is the only scene when the Godfather expressed his hopes and dreams for his son Michael.

Left and opposite: The aging Godfather transfers power to Michael, and becomes his counselor.

Opposite: Discussing the meaning of the lines.

Below: Al Pacino learning the rhythm and nuances of the script.

Pages 236–237: The Godfather hoped that Michael would become a senator or governor or something similar, but it is too late now.

"The Death Of Don Vito"

"The time is past for guns and killings and massacres. We have
to be cunning like the businesspeople; there's more money in it
and it's better for our children and our grandchildren."

DON VITO CORLEONE

"There is a difference between the Mafia as
it really is and the Mafia as we depict it."

— FRANCIS FORD COPPOLA

Page 238: At the end of his life, the kindly Godfather acts like a monster to scare his young grandson.

Pages 240 and 241: Don Vito relaxing.

Below: Coppola, Brando, Anthony Gounaris, and his mother get to know each other.

Opposite: Anthony Corleone (Anthony Gounaris) is momentarily frightened when his grandfather puts orange peel in his mouth and roars.

"Brando's death scene was very self-indulgent, in that it didn't just say what it had to say and get out. It was like four minutes with this little kid. That's the best scene in the film, I think."

— FRANCIS FORD COPPOLA

Opposite and pages 246–247: Grandfather and grandson playing among the tomato vines.

Page 248: The Godfather at rest.

Page 249: Michael enacts his revenge on the Five Families during the baptism of his son. This is the corpse of Don Philip Tattaglia (Victor Rendina).

Pages 250–251: Don Michael Corleone, the new head of the family, accepts the tributes of his *caporegimes*.

"If Cosa Nostra had been black or socialist, Corleone would have been dead or in jail. But because the Mafia patterned itself so closely on the corporation, and dealt in a hard-nosed way with money, and with politics, it prospered. The Mafia is so . . . *American!*"

— MARLON BRANDO

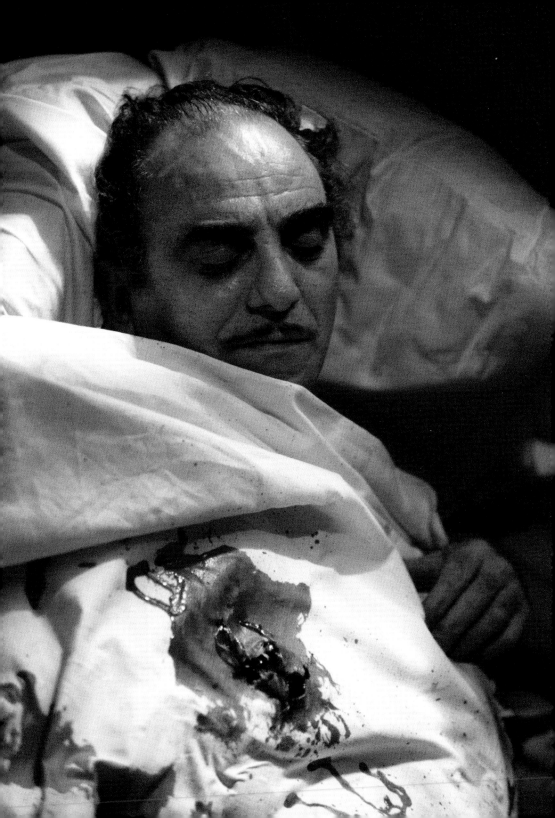

The Godfather Part II

"He Will Grow Strong"

"I want to show how two men, father and son, were born into the world innocent, and how they were corrupted by this Sicilian waltz of vengeance."

FRANCIS FORD COPPOLA

Pages 254–255: Don Michael Corleone (Al Pacino) is the head of a large and powerful organization.

Page 256: In 1901, Vito Andolini (Oreste Baldini) arrives in America.

Pages 258–259: Some townspeople from Corleone help Vito escape from Don Ciccio, who has ordered all the Andolinis to be killed, having already killed Vito's father, mother, and brother.

Opposite: The Ellis Island scenes were filmed at the fish market in Trieste, Italy.

Right: Vito is given the surname Corleone, after his hometown.

Pages 262–263: Director Francis Ford Coppola with Oreste Baldini during the examination scene. Vito has smallpox and is quarantined for three months.

"I Trust These Men
With My Life"

"In *Part II*, once and for all, I wanted to destroy
the Corleone family, and make it clear that
Michael was a cold-hearted bastard murderer."

FRANCIS FORD COPPOLA

"You know something, those dagos are crazy when it comes to their wives."

— DEANNA CORLEONE

Page 264: In 1958, Michael and his wife, Kay, are attacked at their Lake Tahoe estate. Somebody close to the family must have betrayed them.

Pages 266–267: Celebrating Anthony Vito Corleone's communion in style at Lake Tahoe.

Left: Connie Corleone (Talia Shire) is recently divorced and planning to marry her latest boyfriend.

Opposite: Fredo Corleone (John Cazale, right) cannot control his drunken wife, Deanna (Mariana Hill).

Page 270: In a New York theater, 1917, Pepino (Livio Giorgi) receives a letter from Naples telling him his mother is dead. He cannot live any longer, puts a gun to his head, and sings *Senza Mamma [Without Mama]*.

"The Black Hand"

"The whole film must be qualified not as a personal piece of work of mine, but as an adaptation of a novel, which had some themes and relationships that are of interest to me."

FRANCIS FORD COPPOLA

Opposite: Kathy Beller (as Carla) looks on as Coppola directs Livio Giorgi.

Below: Don Fanucci (Gaston Moschin) threatens Carla to extort protection money from the impresario (Ezio Flagello).

Pages 274–275: The play extols the virtues of arriving in America, the land of dreams.

"Everyone knows that sequels are usually cheap imitations of their parent. I thought it would be exciting if I could reverse that: make a film that was more ambitious, more beautiful . . . more advanced than the first." — FRANCIS FORD COPPOLA

Pages 276–277: Three thugs attack Fanucci in this deleted scene.

Opposite: While delivering groceries, Vito Corleone (Robert De Niro) witnesses an attack on Fanucci.

Right: Fanucci's throat is cut, but he survives. Seeing this, Vito knows that Fanucci is vulnerable and can be defeated.

"Good Health Is The Most Important Thing"

"You're a wise and considerate young man."

HYMAN ROTH

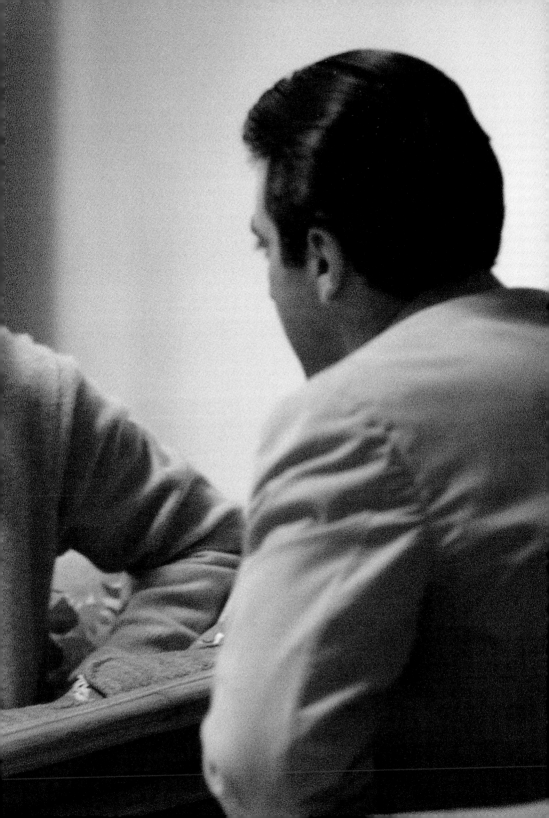

Page 280: Don Michael Corleone in Hyman Roth's home in Miami, Florida.

Pages 282–283: Jewish gangster Hyman Roth (Lee Strasberg) has big plans that involve money from the Corleone family.

Below: Michael lets Roth know that there will be bloodshed because of the attack on his house and family.

Opposite: Lee Strasberg was the artistic director of the Actors Studio, home of "the Method," whose students included Al Pacino, James Dean, Paul Newman, Dustin Hoffman, and many others.

"You're a great man, Mr. Roth.
There's much I can learn from you."
— DON MICHAEL CORLEONE

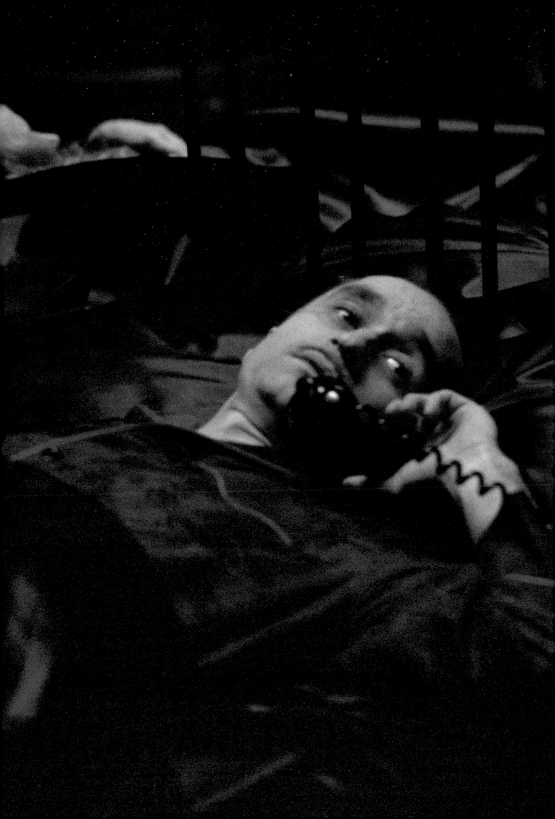

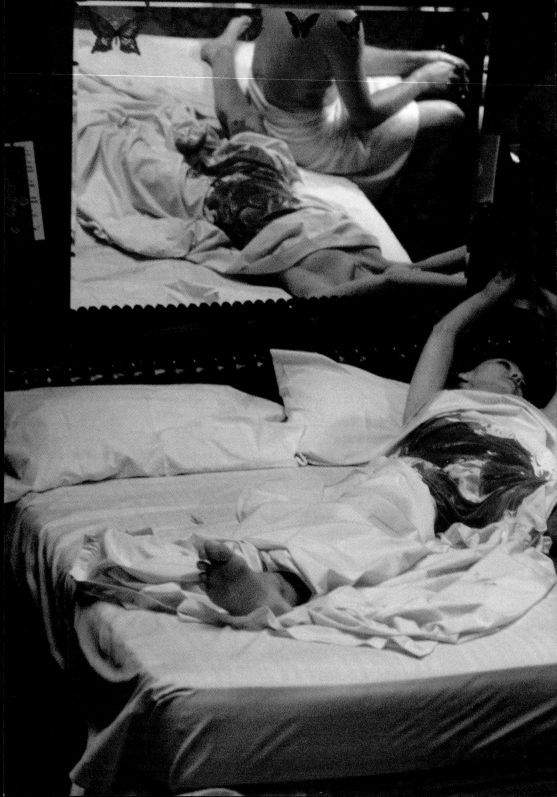

"This girl has no family — nobody knows that she worked here. It'll be as if she never existed. All that's left is our friendship."

— TOM HAGEN

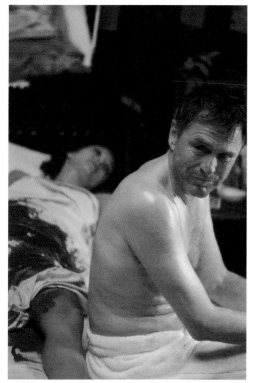

Pages 286–287: Fredo receives a phone call from Johnny Ola, Roth's right-hand man. Fredo is the mole who betrayed Michael.

Pages 288–289: Senator Pat Geary (G. D. Spradlin) wakes up to find his prostitute dead in the bed.

Left: The senator is confused and believes that he has killed the girl.

Opposite: Fredo in one of his Nevada brothels, where the senator is framed for murder so that he will work for the Corleone family.

Pages 292–293: Fredo lives a glamorous life running a casino and bedding showgirls two at a time.

Below: Coppola cannot resist playing the one-armed bandits between setups in Las Vegas.

Opposite: John Cazale was a talented and sensitive actor who died of bone cancer in 1978. All five films he appeared in were nominated for the Academy Award for Best Picture.

The *Playboy* Interview: Al Pacino

INTERVIEW BY LAWRENCE GROBEL
EXCERPTED FROM *PLAYBOY*, DECEMBER 1979

Al Pacino is pacing in his camper, parked on Waverly Place in Greenwich Village, the location for the day's shooting of his latest, and most controversial, picture, *Cruising*. While waiting for director William Friedkin to set up the next shot, he tries to relax by reading aloud all the parts from Bertolt Brecht's *The Resistible Rise of Arturo Ui* to his hairstylist, secretary, and makeup man. Down the street, behind a police barricade, he can hear the faint shouts and the shrill whistles of the gay activists who have gathered to protest the making of this picture, which deals with homosexual murders.

"There they go," Pacino says, interrupting his reading. "Sounds like day crickets." The people in the camper smile, but no one is laughing, especially Pacino, who has found himself in the midst of a controversy he doesn't understand. All his life he has shied away from social movements, political issues, marches, protests. Then, last summer, he did *Richard III* on Broadway — the first Richard done on Broadway in 30 years — and many of the critics attacked him so fiercely it seemed vindictive. No sooner did that play complete its run than *Cruising* began. And, once again, the press was provoked. For an actor who considers himself removed from such furor, and a man who has passionately avoided the press, the spotlight has suddenly been turned strongly his way — and this is the only major interview he has ever granted.

Alfredo James Pacino has traveled a great distance from the South Bronx of his childhood to the Upper East Side of Manhattan, where he lives today. He was born April 25, 1940. His father left his mother when he was two, and he was raised by a protective mother and grandparents.

Nicknamed "Sonny," his friends often called him "The Actor," and, though a prankster throughout his school years, in junior high he was voted most likely to succeed, mainly in recognition of his acting abilities. But what he really wanted to be was a baseball player. When they started teaching Stanislavsky's acting principles (the Method) at the High School of Performing Arts, which he attended, he thought nothing could be more boring. He made it only through his sophomore year before the money ran out and the pressure to get a job surpassed the need to continue his education.

The succession of jobs brought him in contact with all kinds of characters. He was a messenger, shoe salesman, supermarket checker, shoe shiner, furniture mover, office boy, fresh-fruit polisher, newsboy. But he also sensed that he could be more, so he auditioned for Lee Strasberg's Actors Studio while a teenager. Rejected but undeterred, he enrolled in another actors' studio, Herbert Berghof's, where he met the man who would become his mentor and closest friend, Charlie Laughton. Laughton not only taught acting and directed him in his first public play (William Saroyan's *Hello Out There*) but he also wrote poetry and introduced him to poets and writers. Pacino was accepted by the Strasberg studio four years later.

In the mid-'60s, he and a friend started writing comedy revues, which they performed in coffeehouses in Greenwich Village. He was also acting in plays in warehouses and basements. He appeared in numerous plays, including *Awake and Sing!* and *America, Hurrah*. In 1966, he received his first recognition in an off-off-Broadway production of *Why Is a Crooked Letter*. Two years later, he won an Obie for Best Actor in an off-Broadway production of *The Indian Wants the Bronx*. The following year, 1969, he was awarded his first Tony — the legitimate theater's Oscar — for his Broadway performance in *Does a Tiger Wear a Necktie?*

Like Marlon Brando after his major stage debut in *A Streetcar Named Desire*, Pacino was lured by Hollywood. He was offered about a dozen pictures before he and his then manager, Marty Bregman, decided to choose *The Panic in Needle Park* (though he did appear in a bit part in a Patty Duke movie called *Me, Natalie*). *Panic* was a strange and disturbing film about a New York drug addict, and has only now picked up a cult following.

There was something, however, about Pacino that made another newcomer in Hollywood, Francis Ford Coppola, choose him for a film he was about to do on the Mafia. Coppola had big ideas. He wanted not only this relatively unknown actor to play a major role in his film but also another actor not considered bankable at the time: Marlon Brando. The studio balked twice, but Coppola insisted. The result was *The Godfather*, a film that reversed the downward trend of Brando's career and that shot Al Pacino into the ranks of stardom.

Nominated for an Academy Award for Best Supporting Actor, Pacino was insulted (he was onscreen longer than Brando, who won — and refused — the Oscar that year) and boycotted the awards ceremony. For his third movie, *Scarecrow*, he chose an offbeat part in which he played a freewheeling rover on the road with an ex-con, played by Gene Hackman. An unsuccessful picture, it became Pacino's most upsetting experience with the movie industry.

Still, he responded with another recognized performance in *Serpico*, the New York cop who exposed the New York police force for taking bribes and almost lost his life for it. This time he was nominated for an Oscar for Best Actor. His third Oscar nomination came after his strongest performance to date, as Michael Corleone in *The Godfather: Part II*. This was the movie that proved that Pacino was among the rare breed of actors who would leave their mark in American cinema history.

It was a controlled and troubling performance, which put him in the hospital for exhaustion halfway through the production. But when it was completed, he signed to do another controversial and memorable film, *Dog Day Afternoon*, in which he played a bisexual bank robber. For the fourth time, he was nominated for an Oscar.

Hollywood continued to recognize his enormous talent, but he was still an outsider. He refused to move to California, preferring to live in a small, unpretentious apartment in Manhattan; and he refused to consider himself solely a movie actor. Pacino feels his roots are in the theater, and he returns whenever the pressures of being a movie "star" become too great.

His next movie was *Bobby Deerfield*, the story of a superstar race-car driver going through an identity crisis. It was also the story of Pacino and his costar, Marthe Keller, who became an item when they decided to extend their relationship offscreen as she moved in with him. But the film didn't work for Pacino or for the public. He decided to return to Broadway to do *Richard III*.

But before he did, he completed one more picture, *...And Justice for All*, directed by Norman Jewison. Just released, it tells the story of an ethical lawyer fighting corruption in the judicial system. Once again, Pacino displays a wide range of acting ability that will almost certainly earn him his fifth Oscar nomination.

While his professional life has turned him into a superstar and a wealthy man (he received over $1 million for *...And Justice for All*), his private life remains somewhat in turmoil. When he was still in his teens, he lived with a woman for a number of years. When they broke up, he lived for short periods with other women, until he met Jill Clayburgh. They lived together for five years. When that broke up (she married playwright David Rabe), he had a relationship with Tuesday Weld, and then with Marthe Keller. That, too, ended about a year and a half ago, and Pacino, who will soon turn 40, remains, like so many of the characters he plays, alone. But his attitude

toward relationships and what he wants out of life is changing, as Lawrence Grobel (whose last *Playboy* interview was with Godfather One, Marlon Brando) discovered. His report:

"My first impression of Pacino's lifestyle brought to mind a line from *Hamlet*: 'I could be bounded in a nutshell and count myself a king of infinite space.' His three-room apartment consists of a small kitchen with worn appliances, a bedroom dominated by an unmade bed and a bathroom whose toilet is always running, and a living room that is furnished like a set for a way-off-off-Broadway production of some down-and-out city dweller. 'I know poor people who live in more luxury than this,' I thought. Which made me instantly like this man, whose material needs are obviously slight. All around the living room were dog-eared paperback copies of Shakespeare's plays and stacks of scripts, including one that Costa-Gavras had recently given him based on André Malraux's *Man's Fate*.

"For the next two weeks, I saw Pacino every evening and some afternoons, our talks often continuing into the early hours of the morning. For an hour or two, he would sit or lie on the couch, then jump up and go into the kitchen to light a cigarette from the stove, check the time, walk around a bit. One night I smelled something burning and we ran into the kitchen to see a pot holder in flames on the stove. Pacino picked up the teakettle and calmly, as if such things happened all the time, put out the fire. On another night, I arrived to find him downstairs in the hall, picking up the pieces of a broken Perrier bottle that he had dropped on his way to the elevator. 'People wouldn't believe I do this, but I do,' he said.

"During our first few meetings, Pacino had trouble completing his thoughts—his mind jumped, his sentences dangled, he spoke in dashes and ellipses. But as we got to know each other, his sentences and thoughts became complete. He was fascinated with the actual process of being interviewed. 'Nobody ever asked me for opinions,' he said.

"We finished the interview on a Saturday and I was scheduled to fly back to L.A. the next evening. Sunday morning, Pacino called, wanting to know when my plane was leaving. When I told him, he said, 'Well, that gives us enough time for one more talk.' I put the batteries back into my tape recorders and grabbed a taxi to his place.

"Finally, it was time to say goodbye. I had 40 hours of talk on tape and close to 2,000 pages of transcription to reduce. 'I feel like I have played ball with you,' Pacino said as I left. 'Like we know the same candy store or we remember that time when we opened a hydrant or something. It is a good feeling.' I smiled and nodded. That was exactly how I felt about him. And I think some of that good feeling comes through in the interview. Along with the doubts and hesitations, which he continued to express over the phone after I arrived in Los Angeles. He may never do another interview, but for this one, Al Pacino definitely was talking."

Pacino: Actually, I'd rather you not put the tape on yet—until I get a little bit warmed up here.

Playboy: It's best to just leave it on and forget about it.

Pacino: Whatever you say. I'm not going to tell you how to do your job. This is so new to me.

Playboy: Do you feel like this is a coming-out for you?

Pacino: Definitely. It is a huge thing, this interview. There's a certain power in these interviews that I haven't found in profiles—a real power.

Marlon Brando, Jane Fonda, they can be taken seriously. I don't know that I can be yet, because I haven't accomplished enough things in my life.

Playboy: After a lifetime of avoiding the press, what made you finally decide to talk?

Pacino: I sort of got tired of saying no, because it gets misread. The reason I haven't before was that I just didn't think that I would be able to do it. But after a while, you just start to feel like, why not? So I've been saying yes much more. I'm tired of being too careful, too protective. Actually, look what yes has done to me. I said yes to *Richard III* and to *Cruising.* No wonder I said no for so many years! [Laughs]

Playboy: Want to change your mind?

Pacino: No, let me try yeses for a while.

Playboy: Do you care how you come off in this?

Pacino: I want to be interesting in an interview just as much as I want to do well in a part.

Playboy: Good. First, though, we're curious: Why do you have Candice Bergen's name on your apartment door and another name on the directory downstairs?

Pacino: For the obvious reasons—to avoid being hassled. She used to live in this apartment, but it doesn't say Candice Bergen, it says C. Bergen. On the directory, I had Goldman for a while, but then a guy named Goldman came in and said, "Stop using my name."

Playboy: We can appreciate your desire to keep a low profile. How many people in this building know you live here?

Pacino: Everybody in the building knows. They are very considerate.

Playboy: From the looks of things in this apartment, it doesn't appear that your star status has gone to your head.

Pacino: My lifestyle changes a lot. I've been here five years, but it's like I'm passing through. On your way to Bombay, you stop here, stay over, and then you keep going. This is the kind of place I have. It's always been that way. I look around at places I think I should be living in, then I come back and move the couch or the piano and I'm satisfied. This is a pretty nice place.

"The less you want things, the more they come to you. If it's meant to be, it will be."
— AL PACINO

Playboy: OK. Let's start on your current film— *...And Justice for All.* How do you feel about it?

Pacino: I sense a certain kind of originality in the way it is done. I have never seen a film like this before.

Playboy: How do you see it?

Pacino: It's a simple picture, really. It's about ethics and people; about a guy who is trying to do his job and his relationship to the law. To say it's about legal systems sounds boring, and that's not what it is. It's funny and poignant.

Playboy: The ending is pretty radical—you sort of watch your character's law career go down the drain in a rather triumphant, perhaps self-indulgent way.

Pacino: Does the audience have a sense of that? I hope they do. That the guy is giving it all up. You are seeing this guy struggle; it's the last time he's going to be up there. What he's trying to do is expose the system.

Below: Pacino and Coppola relaxing
on location in the Dominican Republic.

Opposite and page 307: Pacino and
Coppola enjoying life at poolside.

Playboy: How much research did you do for
the part?

Pacino: I researched it a lot. I did a lot of
work with lawyers before filming began, so I
felt kind of close to the courts. At one point
recently, a friend said to me he was having
trouble with a contract and I just instinctively
said, "Let me see that." You get the feeling
that you are able to do these things. It is
crazy. I literally took it from him and began
to give him a legal opinion. Can you imagine
that?

Playboy. Didn't you also do something like that
when you played Serpico? Try to arrest a truck
driver?

Pacino: Yeah, I tried to. It was a hot summer
day and I was in the back of a cab. There was
this truck farting all that stuff in my face. I
yelled out, "Why are you putting that crap in
the street?" He said, "Who are you?" I yelled,
"I am a cop and you are under arrest, pull
over!" I pulled out my Serpico badge. It was a
fantasy for a moment. I told him I would put
him under citizen's arrest, but then I realized
what I was doing.

Playboy: Have you gotten carried away like that in
any of your other pictures?

Pacino: Let me see. In *The Panic in Needle Park*,
I was playing the part of someone dealing dope
on a street corner—and there was a guy actually

dealing heroin right there. I looked at him, he
looked at me, and I got real confused.

Playboy: Panic was your first film—were you
very selective in choosing that?

Pacino: I turned down a lot of films before I made
my first one. I knew that it was time for me to
get into movies. I didn't know what it would
be. When *The Panic in Needle Park* came along,

Marty Bregman pushed and helped get it together. Without him, I don't know what I would have done. He is directly responsible for five movies. He was just a great influence on my career.

Playboy: How did Bregman become your manager?

Pacino: He saw me in an off-Broadway show and said that he was willing to back me with anything I wanted to do. I didn't quite know what he was talking about. Then he said that he would sponsor me. I still didn't know what he meant. As it turned out, he acted as a go-between for myself and the business. It was a very important relationship. He acted as an insulator. He got me to work. Encouraged me to do *The Godfather. Serpico* was completely his idea. He got me to do *Dog Day.*

Playboy: Did you have a formal contract with him?

Pacino: Yes, I did. And it was expensive, but it was certainly worth it.

Playboy: You're no longer with him?

Pacino: No. Our relationship changed several years ago, then it just finally dissipated. He became a producer. It wasn't the same anymore.

Playboy: Getting back to *Panic*, what did you think when you first saw yourself larger than life?

Pacino: I was drunk when I saw the first screening, but I was surprised at my bounciness, that I was all over the place. I did say, though, "That's a talented actor, but he needs work. Help. And he needs to work. And learn. But there's talent there." I don't like to go on about myself. I feel sometimes that it's not me who has something to offer but, hopefully, my talent.

Playboy: Well, unless your talent talks, you're going to have to go on about yourself.

Pacino: [Getting up] Mind if I stand and talk to you? Walk around a bit? I wonder if it's a competition thing, an interview. Does it become a battle or a cat-and-mouse thing? But it's probably impossible to strip my defenses. How could I do that with anybody?

Playboy: Are you feeling very defensive now?

Pacino: I'm in a . . . certain kind of condition now.

Playboy: Strained?

Pacino: Stained.

Playboy: Why don't we talk about it? It must have something to do with the fact that you've been filming *Cruising* in New York City and the set has been picketed and harassed. Gay activists have claimed the story is antihomosexual.

Pacino: I feel I don't know what's going on. I don't understand it. It's the first time in my life I've ever been in this position.

Playboy: You play a cop who tracks down a killer of homosexuals, and some of the protests have been about the fact that the film shows scenes on the sadomasochistic fringes of gay life, rather than the mainstream of homosexual life.

"I remember that when I first met in a restaurant with Francis to discuss doing *Godfather II*, I left absolutely filled with his inspiration; he just charged me with electricity." — AL PACINO

Pacino: That's the point! When I first read the script, I didn't even know those fringes existed. But it's just a fragment of the gay community, the same way the Mafia is a fragment of Italian-American life.

Playboy: What does the film seem to you to be about?

Pacino: It's a film about ambivalence. I thought the script read partly like Pinter, partly like Hitchcock, a whodunit, an adventure story.

Playboy: Apparently, the gay community in New York sees it differently. Pamphlets were distributed calling the film "a rip-off" that uses gay male stereotypes as the backdrop for a story about a murderer of homosexuals.

Pacino: How can they say that without seeing the movie?

Playboy: But how do you react to the charges?

Pacino: Well, it makes me feel bad. It's actually hard for me to respond at all. When I read the screenplay, the thought of its being anti-gay never even came to me. It never dawned on me that it would provoke those kinds of feelings. I'm coming from a straight point of view, and maybe I'm not sensitive enough in that area. But they are sensitive to the situation, and I can't argue with that. The only thing I can say is that it isn't a movie yet. It has not been put together as a movie.

Playboy: Do you think those protests will have an effect on the outcome of the film?

Pacino: If the gay community feels the film shows them in a bad light, then it is good they are protesting, because anything that raises consciousness in this area is all right. But I hope that's not the case. When I saw *The Deer Hunter*, my only reaction to some of the war scenes in Vietnam was: War is tough; I don't want to be there. I was taken by a general wave of feeling and swept up in the horror of war. But I wasn't thinking that the film was racist, as many accused it of being. If I had been preconditioned to think it was racist, I probably would have read that into it, too.

Playboy: Is *Cruising* your most controversial project?

Pacino: There is no second to it. I thought *Dog Day* was going to be, but nobody bothered us on the set. Nothing else even comes close.

Playboy: Don't you feel a responsibility for some of the issues the movie raises, since it's an Al Pacino movie?

Pacino: You're turning this into an Al Pacino movie? Al Pacino is an actor in this movie. The way the press focuses attention on something like this is by throwing my name into it. Responsibilities are relative. My responsibility is to a character in a script, to a part I'm playing—not to an issue I'm unqualified to discuss.

Playboy: But aren't we all ultimately responsible for what we do? Isn't what you're saying something of a cop-out?

Pacino: I don't think the film is anti-gay, but I can only repeat — I'm responsible for giving the best performance I can. I took this role because the character is fascinating, a man who is ambiguous both morally and sexually; he's both an observer and a provocateur. It gave me an opportunity to paint a character impressionistically — a character who is something of a blur. I also took the role because Billy Friedkin is one of the best directors working today.

My communication with the public is as an actor. Although I'd never want to do anything to harm the gay community — or the Italian-American community or the police community or any group I happen to represent onscreen — I can only respond in my capacity as an actor.

Playboy: Since you're halfway through the filming, what's your sense of the movie so far?

Pacino: There's a power to it, a certain theatricality, no doubt about that. I sensed it when I read it and I can feel it while we're shooting it.

I hope Billy's energy comes off on the screen. It's extraordinary to be around him. It's like a temple he's creating, and it lifts you. He's a lot like Coppola in that way.

Playboy: How is that?

Pacino: I remember that when I first met in a restaurant with Francis to discuss doing *Godfather II*, I left absolutely filled with his inspiration; he just charged me with electricity. I wasn't going to do *Godfather II*. There's a funny story about how much they were going to pay me for *Godfather II*, before Francis convinced me. It's about how I got that first big salary everybody talks about.

Playboy: How did you get it?

Pacino: They wanted to give me a hundred grand on the second picture, and even I knew that was … They said, "How about a hundred and fifty?" I said, "Well, I don't think so." They said, "How about if Puzo writes the screenplay?" I said sure. Mario wrote a screenplay, I read it and it was OK, but it wasn't … So I said no. They went up to two. I said no. Then they went to two-fifty and three and three-fifty. Then they made a big jump and went to four-fifty. And I said no. Then they called me into the office in New York. There was a bottle of J&B on the table. We began drinking, talking, laughing, and the producer opened his drawer and he pulled out a tin box. I was sitting on the other side and he pushed it over in my direction. He said, "What if I were to tell you that there was $1 million in cash there?" I said, "It doesn't mean anything — it's an abstraction." It was the damnedest thing: I ended up kind of apologizing to the guy for not taking the million.

Playboy: He was obviously making you an offer as if you were really the Mafia character you played. What made you change your mind?

Pacino: Francis told me about the script. He was so wigged out by the prospect of doing it, he would inspire anybody. The hairs on my head

stood up. You can feel that sometimes with a director. I usually say, if you feel that from a director, go with him.

Playboy: Let's finish the story. You didn't get $1 million for it, you got $600,000 and 10 percent of the picture; is that correct?

Pacino: I think so.

Playboy: You didn't go to $1 million until *Bobby Deerfield*, right?

Pacino: Yeah.

Playboy: And what did you get for the first *Godfather*?

Pacino: For the first one, I got $35,000. About $15,000 I owed in legal fees.

Playboy: For what?

Pacino: I was involved in a movie called *The Gang That Couldn't Shoot Straight* at MGM. I can't talk too much about it, because I don't know the details. My lawyer is taking care of it, but I was supposed to have said yes and signed for it, and then *The Godfather* came along. Nobody wanted me for *The Godfather*; I guess they wanted to cast Jack Nicholson. My agents were telling me to stick with *The Gang That Couldn't Shoot Straight.* I said, "Well, I don't know, Francis keeps telling me not to go with another picture." It was very nerve-racking. I remember saying to Francis, "I

don't want to be around where I'm not wanted, so please, Francis, no more auditions, no more screen tests, I can live without this picture." He said, "No, you must play it."

Playboy: And then, after the picture was made, MGM got its lawyers after you?

Pacino: Naturally. After *Godfather II*, the MGM people remembered their lawsuit against me and said I owed them a picture. It was a real crazy legal battle that was costing me hundreds of thousands of dollars. There were depositions — "What color tie did he wear when he told you that?" This craziness. Reams and reams of paper. I finally said, "There's something really wrong here," so I simply made a call to the head of MGM and asked him, "What's going on? This is in the hands of lawyers now, there's no dialogue here, what's up?" He and I talked face to face about the situation and we settled the whole thing. The situation was humanized. Sometimes you're fighting against corporations and you can easily forget that people can talk to each other.

Playboy: How did you settle it?

Pacino: Amicably. If a project comes along, we'll work out something. Any project that I find encouraging that isn't attached to a studio, I can go to them, which I definitely would. There's no more paying the lawyers. There's a time to stay out of your affairs and a time to get into them. You have to take an interest in what you do.

"It was the most difficult part I've ever played." — AL PACINO

Playboy: Even when you don't understand what's going on?

Pacino: What happens is you get an inferiority complex, because you don't feel qualified to deal with those situations and you just sort of stand there and look around and nod your head. They say, "Right?" And you say, "Yeah." And you don't know what you're saying. You don't even listen. You pretend to listen. But you've got to learn what's going down — it's like the streets, in a sense.

Playboy: We imagine you didn't stay long with the agents who had told you to forget *The Godfather*.

Pacino: I changed agents. I did it on my own. There was a period where I didn't have an agent and I called William Morris. I said, "Can I speak to the William Morris people? I'm looking for an agent." She said, "Oh? What's your name?" I said, "Al Pacino." She said, "Are you sure?"

Playboy: Getting back to *The Godfather*, Coppola called you self-destructive after your first screen test. Why?

Pacino: Well, he was expecting me to do more in a scene. He took the dullest scene that Michael had, the first wedding scene, which is an exposition scene, and I did it and he wanted me to do more. I don't know what he expected me to do. He tested people with the wrong scene. At first I thought he wanted me for Sonny. At the time, I didn't care if I got the

Above: A carefree Pacino in contrast to his intense role.

part or not. The less you want things, the more they come to you. If it's meant to be, it will be. Every time I've stuffed or forced something, it hasn't been right.

Playboy: Yet you always knew you'd get the part, didn't you?

Pacino: You just get a sense of things sometimes.

You just know it. It's kind of simple to assess something if you allow it to happen. It's when the ego and greed get in the way that it's harder to assess what the situation is. But if you step back and you take a look at it, you can sense what's going to happen. If I hadn't gotten the *Godfather* role, it would have surprised me, frankly.

Playboy: Did Coppola have you in mind before or after he had decided on Brando?

Pacino: He had Brando in his mind first, I'm sure. We were together at a party and Francis said to me, "Who do you think the Godfather should be?" I said Brando. Francis is extraordinary in that way. He just feels you out. He's a strange kind of man. He's a voyeur that way. I never saw the likes of him. He can detach like nobody I've ever seen. For a man that emotionally powerful to be able to detach the way he does...like Michael Corleone. That's why Francis understood that character.

Playboy: Did you have Francis in mind when you played Michael?

Pacino: Partly I did Francis, partly I modeled him from several people I know.

Playboy: What about any real Mob figures? Did you ever meet any of the Mafia?

Pacino: Yeah. Privately. Somebody gave me a reference.

Playboy: So you could observe them?

Pacino: Observe them, yes.

Playboy: And they let you?

Pacino: Yes.

Playboy: And what happened?

Pacino: Nothing.

Playboy: Are they all still alive?

Pacino: I can't answer that.

Playboy: Is what we saw on the screen styled after what you observed?

Pacino: Ah, no. It wasn't.

Playboy: Where did you meet? At a restaurant?

Pacino: Ah...in the sky. Space Station 22.

Playboy: Right. What were you trying to capture when you played Michael?

Pacino: In the first *Godfather*, the thing that I was after was to create some kind of enigma, an enigmatic-type person. So you felt that we were looking at that person and didn't quite know him. When you see Michael in some of those scenes looking wrapped up in a kind of trance, as if his mind were completely filled with thoughts, that's what I was doing. I was actually listening to Stravinsky on the set, so I'd have that look. I felt that that was the drama in the character, that that was the only thing that was going to make him dramatic. Otherwise, it could be dull. I never worked on a role quite like that. It was the most difficult part I've ever played.

Playboy: There are numerous stories of actors performing with Brando for the first time. What's your feeling about him?

Pacino: There's no doubt every time I see Brando that I'm looking at a great actor. Whether he's doing great acting or not, you're seeing somebody who is in the tradition of a great actor. What he does with it, that's something else, but he's got it all. The talent, the instrument is there, that's why he has endured. I remember when I first saw *On the Waterfront*. I had to see it again, right there. I couldn't move, I couldn't leave the theater. I had never seen the likes of it. I couldn't believe it.

Playboy: What was your first meeting like?

Pacino: Well, Diane Keaton was at that first meeting. We went in and sat at a table and everybody was pretending that he was just another actor, even though we were all nervous. But Diane was open enough to admit how she felt. She sat at the table and Brando said hello to me and to Diane. And Diane said, "Yeah, right, sure," as if she couldn't believe it. She really did it. She said, "I just cannot take that."

Playboy: And afterward?

Pacino: You can't imagine my feelings during the first rehearsal with Brando. It was Jimmy Caan and Bobby Duvall and me, all sitting around, and there's Brando going on about the Indians. Francis is saying to himself, "This is the first rehearsal, what's going to happen tomorrow? We have two more weeks of this." And Duvall was making these faces. I had to leave and sit on the bed, because I was laughing and I didn't want to have Brando think we were laughing at him. Duvall finally said, "Keep talking, Marlon, none of us want to work, just keep talking." With that, Marlon laughed.

I will never forget Brando the first time I did a scene with Keaton. He came and stood right in front of the camera and watched. During the scene at the table, a leaf fell off the tree onto my shoulder. I took off the leaf and tossed it and later Brando said, "I like what you did with the leaf." Afterward, Diane and I just got drunk. But Brando was wonderful to me. He made me laugh, the things he'd do. I'd be playing a scene, and he'd show up off-camera, straight-faced, with a silly fake bird in his pocket. His support was so powerful, it helped me a great deal. What can you say about someone that gracious? He made it so easy.

Playboy: People have said that artistically, you are Brando's godson.

Pacino: People have said that. I don't feel

anywhere near that. It's meaningless, like saying I have green hair.

Playboy: There's a rare quote attributed to you about *Godfather:* "They may have come to see Brando, but they left remembering me." Did you say that?

Pacino: I never said that.

Playboy: Did you have a good time making the *Godfather* films?

Pacino: Actually, except for Francis, I felt really unwanted on the set. And except for Al Ruddy, who was incredibly helpful and good. And with Francis, although I had personality differences with him, those were his performances, he made them. And he knew it. He'd say, "I created you — you're my Frankenstein monster." Another time, he put me in elevator shoes and said, "What's wrong with you? You're walking like Donald Duck!" I said, "Get those lifts out of my shoes and I may move straighter."

Playboy: In fact, you did walk and move differently as Michael, didn't you?

Pacino: I had to move in a different way than I've ever moved before. All heavy. Especially in *II*.

Playboy: Do you have a favorite scene in either of the *Godfather* films — a moment you're particularly proud of?

Pacino: I have one moment in *Godfather II*, nobody sees it. Michael and his sad brother Fredo are in Cuba, seeing the Superman show in the nightclub, and Fredo tells Michael, "Johnny always used to take me here." And you see in that moment that Michael realizes his brother betrayed him. That's my favorite moment, but it's subtle. After the scene, I was taken to the hospital, the next day.

Playboy: From exhaustion?

Pacino: Yeah. We were shooting in the Dominican Republic and I was being treated like a prince or something. Eight bodyguards and all, which was unnecessary. It was very disconcerting. I got physically ill. I was just overworking in that part.

Playboy: How would you rate that part against the others you've played?

Pacino: Of all the parts, I'm most satisfied with *Godfather II*. It was the most important.

Playboy: Is there a *Godfather III* in the future?

Pacino: There was a scene, which was only half shot, where Michael's son comes back to visit him. The kid talks about how he wanted to join the family business. And I tell him that he should give it more time. But they didn't shoot it all, which I found hard to believe.

Playboy: Why didn't they shoot it?

Pacino: We lost the light. Maybe if we hadn't, we'd be hearing about *Godfather III*.

Playboy: Perhaps it's a good thing, because you followed that with another remarkable performance in *Dog Day Afternoon*.

Pacino: You know I almost never got to do that film?

Playboy: Why?

Pacino: I quit once. Dustin Hoffman was going to do it. I was the original one, and then Dustin, and then it went back to me.

Playboy: Why did you quit it?

Pacino: I had just done *Godfather II* and I was tired of films. I just didn't want to make a movie. I found it a hassle. I had done years of stage and I thought I was one of those actors who couldn't adjust to film, because it was too laborious. I guess I was just too tough on myself. I was working in a medium I didn't know and I felt unsure.

Playboy: Why did you decide to do it?

Pacino: Because Frank Pierson wrote a terrific screenplay. And I had strong feelings for that kind of character. See, there're three reasons I take a screenplay: the director, text, and character. If I relate greatly to the director, the text is pretty good, and I think I can do something with the character, I might take it. Or if I can relate greatly to the character and the text and director are OK, I'll take it, too. As long as there's one really strong positive in it. That's how I pick things now. Before, all three had to be great.

Above: Michael Corleone begins to show signs of his physical degeneration.

Playboy: Is that how you felt about the script, the character, and the director, Sidney Lumet, of *Dog Day Afternoon*?

Pacino: Yeah. Pierson had structured it quite beautifully, he really made it sing, it was alive. And Sidney Lumet is a genius in staging; he never tells you a word; just by the way he has you move, the scene comes alive. He pointed me in a direction

made it the kind of film that got received universally.

Playboy: Which moment?

Pacino: When the delivery boy delivers the pizza and then turns around to the crowd and says, in effect, "I'm a star!" It hit right where we're at — the kind of energy wrapped up in the media and with imagery and fantasy and film. We don't know

and said, "Go here and go there." It's extraordinary.

Playboy: There's a truly memorable scene in that film where you come out of the bank screaming "Attica! Attica!" Was that an important scene to you?

Pacino: Yeah, I sensed that kind of rush. Lumet helped me with that. He said, "It's his day in the sun, with all those people out there." Charging at windmills, somebody once said to me. But there's another moment that, I think,

Above: Whilst riding through Havana, Michael sees that the rebels are willing to sacrifice themselves for their freedom.

enough about media yet. We don't know its effect on us. It's new. It's got to do something to us.

Playboy: Did you sense that *Dog Day* was an explosive kind of picture?

Pacino: Yes. My friend Charlie Laughton saw the film and said to me, "Al, do you know what it is like? It is like pulling a pin out of a hand grenade and waiting for it to explode." I remember Lumet saying to me at one point, "It is out of my hands. It has got its own life."

Playboy: Have you felt that with any other picture?

Pacino: With *Serpico*. It had that kind of pace.

Playboy: What drew you to that picture?

Pacino: I read the treatment and thought, "Another cop picture." Then Waldo Salt came over with a screenplay that I could relate to and I was there. Then I met Frank Serpico. The moment I shook his hand and looked into his eyes, I understood what that movie could be. I thought there was something there that I could play.

Playboy: Did you prepare for the part by hanging out with him?

Pacino: Yes. I went out with the cops one night, did about five minutes of that and said, "I can't do this stuff." So I would just sort of hang around Frank, long enough to sort of feel like him. One time we were out at my rented beach house in Montauk. We were sitting there looking at the water. And I thought, "Well, I might as well be like everybody else and ask a silly question," which was, "Why, Frank? Why did you do it?" He said, "Well, Al, I don't know. I guess I have to say it would be because … if I didn't, who would I be when I listened to a piece of music?" I mean, what a way of putting it! That's the kind of guy he was. I enjoyed being with him. There was mischief in his eyes.

Playboy: Frank Serpico is living by himself on a farm in Holland. Is the piece we saw together on one of the TV news-magazine shows the same man you knew?

Pacino: No. That was what was so shocking. He looked as if he didn't belong there. Not natural.

Playboy: He seemed to possess a certain resigned wisdom.

Pacino: Yes. Resigned wisdom — he would laugh at that. He is a funny kind of guy. He was a loner. A man of intelligence. He'll be back on the police force.

"Of all parts I am most satisfied with *Godfather II*. It was the most important."
— AL PACINO

Playboy: Pauline Kael, in her review of *Serpico*, wrote that as you grew your beard, she couldn't distinguish you from Dustin Hoffman.

Pacino: Is that after she had the shot glass removed from her throat?

Playboy: Is that really insulting to you?

Pacino: Why did you ask me that question?

Playboy: To piss you off. [Laughter]

Pacino: Really. I'm too good, right. I'm really too nice.

Playboy: We'll find out.

Pacino: We got time. If somebody says something like that, I can't retort to it. It has to do with what was going through her head at the time. It seems beside the point.

Playboy: Kael wrote, "Pacino's poker face and offhand fast throwaways keep the character remote."

Pacino: Are you kidding me or what? Why was she pissed at me, I wonder? Sometimes the things that piss people off … Well, I piss myself off, too, sometimes. When I've seen myself onscreen from time to time, I've said, "Who does he think he is, smirking like that?" Or, "Why doesn't he take a bath?" But that film seemed pretty good to me.

Playboy: What other films seem pretty good to you?

Pacino: Bang the Drum Slowly is my all-time-favorite film. I saw that three or four times. I'd like to go see it again. The baseball motif, the quality of the relationship between Moriarty and De Niro, is beautiful. Maybe I relate to it because I wanted to be a baseball player. For some reason, people don't talk about that movie.

Playboy: You and De Niro are friends, aren't you?

Pacino: Yeah, I know Bobby pretty well. He's a friend. He and I have gone through similar things. There was a period in my life when it was very important that I get together with somebody I could identify with.

Playboy: Those must have been strange conversations, since neither of you is very talkative. How did you communicate at first?

Pacino: Sign language.

Playboy: That's probably what the press would have to do to interview him.

Pacino: He's always very quiet, it's an inherent thing. He's really honest about that. I think that the press respects that. They don't push him. He does talk with me, though.

Playboy: Do you see any similarities between you and De Niro professionally?

Pacino: I can only judge by what I see on film. I don't see similarities between me and Bobby.

The same thing with Dustin; I don't see it, although I think he's great.

Playboy: What other films besides *Bang the Drum Slowly* do you like?

Pacino: I liked *Viva Zapata.* I liked Gielgud in *The Charge of the Light Brigade.* I liked *The Loves of Isadora* with Vanessa Redgrave; she's a great actress. I loved Nick Nolte in *North Dallas Forty.* I like going to see Olivier. And Walter Matthau, I go to see all his movies. When I first saw *8 1/2*, I liked it a lot. I loved *La Strada.* I wasn't crazy about *Amarcord.* I don't like the Bond films.

Playboy: How did you feel when you saw *Saturday Night Fever* and spotted the poster of yourself — in your Serpico beard — on the wall of John Travolta's room?

Pacino: I ducked. I was watching the screen and I muttered, "That's not Al Pacino, that's Serpico." Sometimes I talk aloud in a movie theater. Like in *The Goodbye Girl*, with Dreyfuss and Marsha Mason, one of the characters says to the other, "Nobody knew Al Pacino before *The Godfather*," and I yelled up at the screen, "You're full of shit, Marsha. You were in a one-act play with me before *The Godfather!*"

Playboy: That was during a regular screening at a movie theater?

Pacino: Yeah. Sometimes I'll do that.

Playboy: Did people turn and stare at you?

Pacino: No, I think Dreyfuss looked down at me from the screen and said, "Shush, Al." [Laughs]

Opposite: Cast and crew befriended many of the locals during the shoot in the Dominican Republic.

"Bigger Than U.S. Steel"

"We will tolerate no guerrillas in casinos,
or the swimming pools."

CUBAN PRESIDENT FULGENCIO BATISTA

Page 320: Hyman Roth is the mastermind behind an enormous investment of criminal money into Cuba.

Pages 322–323: Cuban president Fulgencio Batista (Tito Alba) proudly displays a gold telephone presented to him by the United Telephone and Telegraph Company.

Below: Michael is not impressed.

Opposite: Michael is sitting around a table with legitimate American businesses (food, mining, sugar, telephone), all of whom want to exploit the Cuban market.

"I want to thank this distinguished group of American industrialists for continuing to work with Cuba." — PRESIDENT BATISTA

Below: Coppola and Pacino between scenes on the streets of the Dominican Republic.

Opposite: Coppola deep in thought.

Pages 328–329: Coppola discusses a scene with Lee Strasberg in a rare screen role.

Pages 330–331: Michael and Hyman Roth are in Havana to do business.

Pages 332–333: Hyman Roth consulting with his business associates, all of whom will receive part of his empire when he dies.

Below and opposite: Roth cuts up his birthday cake and gives each of them a piece of it. He names Michael as his successor.

Pages 336–337: Roth is upset that Michael is putting doubt into the other investors by talking about the rebels.

Pages 338–339: Roth is also upset that Michael has not delivered the $2 million he promised.

"When a novelist takes on an ambitious theme, he works on it for two years. I had to write the script for *Godfather II* in three months and then go right into preproduction. I was making a $13-million movie as if it were a Roger Corman picture." — FRANCIS FORD COPPOLA

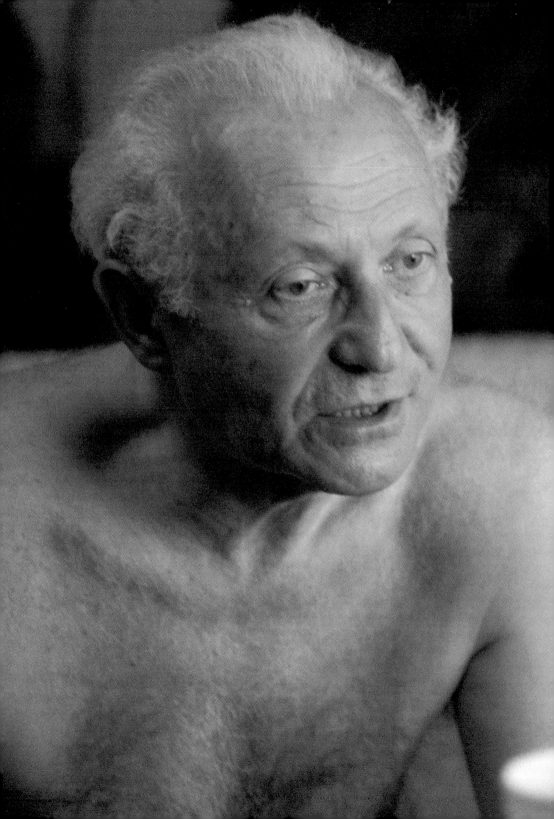

"Assure Him That There Will Be No Reprisals"

"I feel that the film works on a cumulative level, and that it makes an extremely moral statement regarding the self-destructive forces set loose when evil acts are performed for the alleged preservation of good."

FRANCIS FORD COPPOLA

"Why didn't we spend time like this before?" — FREDO CORLEONE

Page 340 and opposite: After Fredo delivers $2 million — a gift for the president — he and Michael go for a drink. It is the first time they have been close for years.

Pages 344–345: New Year's Eve: Fredo and Michael go out on the town protected by Michael's bodyguard (Amerigo Tot).

"Michael and his sad brother Fredo are in Cuba, seeing the Superman show in the nightclub, and Fredo tells Michael, 'Johnny always used to take me here.' And you see in that moment that Michael realizes his brother betrayed him. That's my favorite moment, but it's subtle."

— AL PACINO

Opposite: Having a good time with Fredo.

Right: Michael knows that Hyman Roth plans to have him assassinated before the night is finished.

Pages 348–349: Fredo (right) denies that he knows Johnny Ola, and then reveals that Johnny showed him this sex club. At this moment, Michael knows that Fredo is the traitor.

Pages 350–351: President Fulgencio Batista's
New Year's Eve party.

Pages 352–353, below and opposite: Michael
tells his brother that he knows he is the traitor.

"I know it was you, Fredo. You broke
my heart — you broke my heart!"

— MICHAEL CORLEONE

Below: Michael starts to make his escape
before he is killed.

Opposite: Michael says that he will not harm
Fredo, but Fredo is too scared to go with him.

Pages 358–359: Celebrations erupt in the
streets as the rebels start to take over Havana.

"It's the kind of role where there is a gradual progression and one is changed, and that's very difficult to do when you are doing the end first and going back and forth, back and forth."

— AL PACINO

Opposite: Michael leaves Cuba without Fredo.

"There's an interesting contrast in the film. Vito kills with his own hands, Michael by remote control, while waiting in a dark room. I think most everyone would agree that Michael's is the more terrible violence."

— FRANCIS FORD COPPOLA

Pages 362–363: Michael with family lawyer Tom Hagen (Robert Duvall) and *caporegime* Al Neri (Richard Bright) in Las Vegas.

Pages 364–365: Even though the attempted assassination of Hyman Roth failed, Michael is more interested in getting Fredo back into the family.

Opposite and right: Michael wants to know if the baby was a boy, but Tom does not know.

Pages 368–369: Tom tells Michael that Kay miscarried and lost their baby.

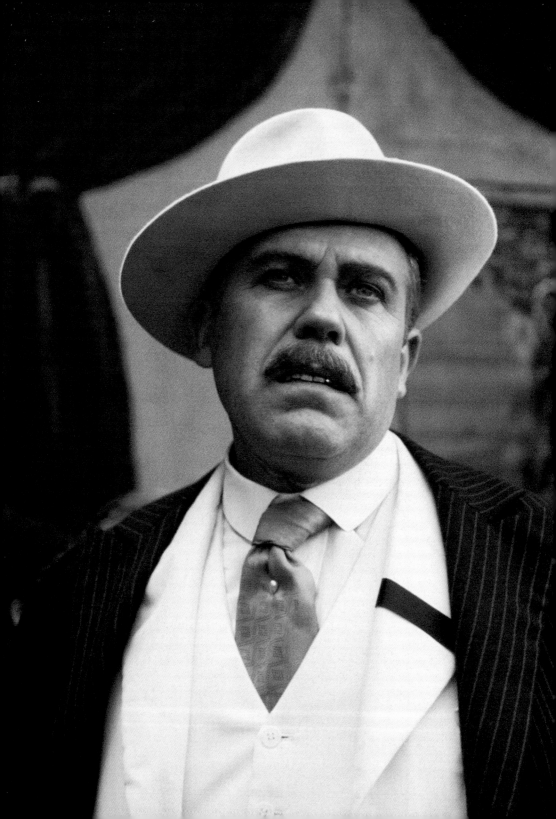

"You Should Let Me Wet My Beak A Little"

"This is my neighborhood. You and your friends should show me some respect."

DON FANUCCI

Page 370: Don Fanucci (Gaston Moschin) is part of The Black Hand, organized extortionists.

Pages 372–373: Now part of Peter Clemenza's gang, Vito waits with a van full of stolen dresses.

Opposite: Vito warms himself in a deleted scene.

Below: Fanucci says that the gang should pay him tribute, and he takes a dress for one of his daughters.

Pages 376–377: Coppola and De Niro filming on the streets of New York.

The *Playboy* Interview: Francis Ford Coppola

INTERVIEW BY WILLIAM MURRAY

EXCERPTED FROM *PLAYBOY*, JULY 1975

"The Godfather was successful beyond my craziest speculation."

— FRANCIS FORD COPPOLA

Playboy: All right, let's start with your recent Oscar haul for *Godfather II.* How did it feel to walk away with so many awards?

Coppola: Two years ago, I went to the Academy Awards ceremonies feeling blasé, not caring. I thought *Godfather I* would win most of the awards, but how important was the Oscar, anyway? Then it became clear that *Cabaret* was running away with the awards, and I suddenly started wanting to win desperately. When I didn't, I got very depressed. I figured I'd never make another film that would win an Oscar; I was going to go off and make small, personal films, the kind that rarely win awards. I had wanted to leave a winner.

This year, I thought *Chinatown* would clean up. I had two pictures nominated — *Godfather II* and *The Conversation* — and I figured that would split my vote. I was intrigued with the idea of losing twice after coming so close, which might be a record in itself. So when it all happened, I was so elated I didn't know what to do. I never expected Best Picture. I felt *Godfather II* was too demanding, too complex. But when it won, I felt the members were telling me they appreciated the fact that we'd tried to make a film with integrity.

Playboy: Your career as a director has been made by the two *Godfather* movies, and most of the critics seem to have recognized what you were trying to do with them, but none has had a kind word for the novel nor for its author, Mario Puzo. *The New Yorker*'s Pauline Kael, in fact,

Page 378: Director Francis Ford Coppola.

Above: The fame of the first *Godfather* film turned the shooting of the second part into a tourist attraction.

380

calls the book trash. Could you have made two fine movies out of trash?

Coppola: When I was first offered the project, I started to read the book and I got only about 50 pages into it. I thought it was a popular, sensational novel, pretty cheap stuff. I got to the part about the singer supposedly modeled on Frank Sinatra and the girl Sonny Corleone liked so much because her vagina was enormous — remember that stuff in the book? It never showed up in the movie. Anyway, I said, "My God, what *is* this — *The Carpetbaggers*?" So I stopped reading it and said, "Forget it."

Four or five months later, I was again offered the opportunity to work on it and by that time, I was in dire financial straits with my own company in San Francisco, so I read further. Then I got into what the book is really about — the story of the family, this father and his sons, and questions of power and succession — and I thought it was a terrific story, if you could cut out all the other stuff. I decided it could be not only a successful movie but also a *good* movie. I wanted to concentrate on the central theme, and that's what I tried to do.

So the fact is, it wasn't a piece of trash. Like me, Mario went after the money at first. He's very frank about that. But if the two movies are strong, it's because of what Mario originally put in his book that was strong and valid. Mario himself, by the way, doesn't think *The Godfather* is his best book, but it's the only one of his novels that sold really well. I have great respect for Mario. He created the story, he created the characters, even in *Part II*, which I wrote more of than *Part I*. But all the key elements go back to his book.

Playboy: Had you heard about *The Godfather* before reading it and hating it?

Coppola: Yes, and it's a strange story. One Sunday afternoon, I was sitting around my home in San Francisco, reading the *New York Times*, and I saw an ad for a new book. Couldn't tell what it was about from the book cover — it looked kind of solemn. I thought it might be an intellectual work by some new Italian author named Mario Puzo, so I clipped the ad. I was just going to inquire about it. Right then, Peter Bart, a friend of mine, came by with someone I'd never met before: Al Ruddy, who later became producer of *The Godfather* but at that time had nothing to do with the project. We started talking and Peter mentioned a book he'd just heard about: *The Godfather*, by Mario Puzo. He explained what it was about. I had no interest in filming a best seller, so I said, "No kidding — I just noticed an ad for it." At that very moment, the phone rang. It was Marlon Brando. I'd contacted him to ask if I might send by the script of *The Conversation*, which I'd written with him in mind. He was just calling to say, "Sure, send the script over."

That all happened in one afternoon. Several months later, Al Ruddy was named producer of *The Godfather*, I received my first offer to direct it, and Marlon Brando would shortly have the lead. It still seems bizarre to me that the various elements came together that day in my home.

Playboy: After *The Godfather* went on to unparalleled success, what got you interested in doing a sequel?

Coppola: Initially, the idea of a sequel seemed horrible to me. It sounded like a tacky spin-off, and I used to joke that the only way I'd do it was if they'd let me film *Abbott and Costello Meet the Godfather* — that would have been fun. Then I entertained some Russian film executives who were visiting San Francisco and they asked me if I was going to make *The Godfather: Part II*. That was the first time I heard the phrase used; I guess you could say I stole the title from the Russians.

In short, it seemed like such a terrible idea that I began to be intrigued by the thought of pulling it off. Simple as that. Sometimes I sit around thinking I'd like to get a job directing a TV soap opera, just to see if I could make it the most wonderful thing of its kind ever done. Or I imagine devoting myself to directing the plays of a cub-scout troop and having it be the most exciting theater in the country. You know that feeling when something seems so outrageous, you just have to do it? That's what happened to me.

Then after I started thinking about the idea, when I considered that we'd have most of the same actors, the scenes we might be able to develop in depth, I started feeling it really might be something innovative.

Playboy: Do you, like some critics, think *Godfather II* is a better film than *Godfather I?*

Coppola: The second film goes much further than the first one. It's much more ambitious and novelistic in its structure. If you get off on the wrong foot with it, I can imagine that it would be like a Chinese water torture to sit through it. But it's a more subtle movie, with its own heartbeat. And it was very tough on some of the actors, especially Al Pacino.

Playboy: Is it true that you had to stop shooting for two or three weeks when you were on location in Santo Domingo because Pacino was exhausted?

Coppola: Yes. The role of Michael is a very strange and difficult one and it put a terrific strain on him. It was like being caught in a kind of vise. In the first picture, he went from being a young, slightly insecure, naive and brilliant young college student to becoming this horrible Mafia killer. In *Godfather II,* he's the same man from beginning to end — working on a much more subtle level, very rarely having a big climactic scene where an actor can unload, like blowing the spittle out of the tube of a trombone. The entire performance had to be kind of vague and so understated that, as an actor, you couldn't really be sure what you were doing. You had the tremendous pressure of not knowing whether your performance would have a true, cumulative effect, whether you were creating a monster or just being terrible. The load on Al was terrific and it really ran him down physically.

Playboy: One of the most important areas you explore in *Godfather II* is the connection between Mafia operations and some of our legitimate big-business interests. Are you saying that some corporations are no better and no worse than organized crime?

Coppola: Right from the very beginning it became clear, as I was doing my research, that though the Mafia was a Sicilian phenomenon, there was no way it could really have flowered except in the soil of America. America was absolutely ripe for the Mafia. Everything the Mafia believed in and was set up to handle — absolute control, the carving out of territories, the rigging of prices, and the elimination of competition — everything was here. In fact, the corporate philosophy that built some of our biggest industries and great personal fortunes was a Mafia philosophy. So when those Italians arrived here, they found themselves in the perfect place.

It became clear to me that there was a wonderful parallel to be drawn, that the career of Michael Corleone was the perfect metaphor for the new land. Like America, Michael began as a clean, brilliant young man endowed with incredible resources and believing in a humanistic idealism. Like America, Michael was the child of an older system, a child of Europe. Like America, Michael was an innocent who had tried to correct the ills and injustices of his progenitors. But then he got blood on his hands. He lied to himself and to others about what he was doing and why. And so he became not only the mirror image of what he'd come from but worse. One of the reasons I wanted to make *Godfather II* is that I wanted to take Michael to what I felt was the logical conclusion. He wins every battle; his brilliance and his resources enable him to defeat all his enemies. I didn't want Michael to die. I didn't want Michael to be put into prison. I didn't want him to be assassinated by his rivals. But, in a bigger sense, I also wanted to destroy Michael. There's no doubt that, by the end of this picture, Michael Corleone, having beaten everyone, is sitting there alone, a living corpse.

Playboy: Is that your metaphor for America today?

Coppola: Unlike America, Michael Corleone is doomed. There's no way that man is ever going to change. I admit I considered some upbeat touch at the end, like having his son turn against him to indicate he wouldn't follow in that tradition, but honesty — and Pacino — wouldn't let me do it. Michael is doomed. But I don't at all feel that America is doomed. I thought it was healthy to make this horror-story statement — as a warning, if you like — but, as a nation, we don't have to go down that same road, and I don't think we will.

Playboy: A number of critics feel that you and others — including, perhaps, *Playboy*, with its series on organized crime — helped romanticize

the Mafia in America. How do you respond to that?

Coppola: Well, first of all, the Mafia was romanticized in the book. And I was filming that book. To do a film about my real opinion of the Mafia would be another thing altogether. But it's a mistake to think I was making a film about the Mafia. *Godfather: Part I* is a romance about a king with three sons. It is a film about power. It could have been the Kennedys. The whole idea of a family living in a compound — that was all based on Hyannis Port. Remember, it wasn't a documentary about Mafia chief Vito Genovese. It was Marlon Brando with Kleenex in his mouth.

Playboy: Where do the films depart most radically from the truth?

Coppola: Where you get into the mythic aspects of the Godfather, the great father who is honorable and will not do business in drugs. The character was a synthesis of Genovese and Joseph Profaci, but Genovese ordered his soldiers not to deal in drugs while he himself did just that on the side; Profaci was dishonorable at a lot of levels. The film Godfather would never double-cross anyone, but the real god-fathers double-crossed people over and over.

Playboy: Still, you won't deny that, whatever your intentions, *Godfather I* had the effect of romanticizing the Mafia?

Coppola: I felt I was making a harsh statement about the Mafia and power at the end of *Godfather I* when Michael murders all those people, then lies to his wife and closes the door. But obviously, many people didn't get the point I was making. And so if the statement I was trying to make was outbalanced by the charismatic aspects of the characters, I felt *Godfather II* was an opportunity to rectify that. The film is pretty rough. The essence of

Godfather I is all Mario Puzo's creation, not mine. With *Godfather II*, which I had a greater part in writing, I emerged a bit to comment on the first film.

But the fact still may be that people *like* Marlon and Jimmy and Al too much. If you were taken inside Adolf Hitler's home, went to his parties, and heard his stories, you'd probably have liked him. If I made a film of Hitler and got some charismatic actor to play him, people would say I was trying to make him a good human being. He wasn't, of course, but the greatest evil on earth is done by sane human beings who are miserable in themselves. My point is that you can't make a movie about what it's like inside a Mafia family without their seeming to be quite human.

Playboy: What about those who say *not* that the Mafia is romanticized but that it simply doesn't exist?

Coppola: When people say the Mafia doesn't exist, in a way they're right. When they say it does exist, they're right, too. You have to look at it with different eyes: It's not a secret Italian organization, as it's portrayed. The most powerful man in the Mafia at one time wasn't Italian — he was a Jew. Meyer Lansky became powerful because he was the best at forging their common interests — that's just good business practice.

Playboy: Except that, as far as we know, AT&T hasn't killed anyone in pursuit of its business.

Coppola: Who says? Who says?

Playboy: Have you got something on AT&T?

Coppola: AT&T I don't know about, but ITT in Chile? I wouldn't bet my life that it hadn't. And it's not just business. How about the Yablonski murders in that coal miners' union? That was just the union equivalent of a Mafia hit. How about politics? Assassination of a president is the quickest way to bring about lasting and enormous social change. What's the difference between the United States' putting a guy like Trujillo in power so our companies can

operate in the Dominican Republic, and the Mafia's handing the Boston territory to one of its *capos*? Then, after 20 years, either guy gets a little uppity and either organization feels free to knock him off.

Playboy: Do you have any stories to tell about how the *real* Mafia reacted to the *Godfather* films?

Coppola: No.

Playboy: And you wouldn't tell if you had any?

Coppola: No, I *would.* But the fact is I got some terrific advice from Mario Puzo. He told me that, in his experience, Mafia guys loved the glamour of show business and that, if you let them, they'd get involved. So Mario told me that I'd probably be contacted and when I was, I should refuse to open up to them. I shouldn't take their phone number, I shouldn't let them feel they could visit me. Because if there's one thing about them, it's that they respect that attitude. If you turn them off, they won't intrude into your life. Al Ruddy, the producer, was out having dinner with a lot of them, but I wouldn't participate in any way whatsoever with them.

Funny thing is, I've never been very interested in the Mafia — even though some important guys in the Mob have the same name as I do. "Trigger Mike" Coppola was one of Vito Genovese's lieutenants, I think. Terrible man.

Playboy: Any relation?

Coppola: You mean Uncle Mike? No, of course not. Coppola is a common Italian name.

Playboy: One Hollywood person who has been mentioned in connection with the Mafia is Frank Sinatra. How are your relations with him, considering that most people believe he was the model for Johnny Fontane, the singer-actor in *The Godfather*?

Coppola: I met Sinatra several times before filming started. They were very friendly meetings, since I never liked the idea of exploiting a fictionalization of a man, any man — and I told him so. I let him know that I didn't like that part of the book and that I'd minimize it in the film. Sinatra was very appreciative. Then he turned to me and said, "I'd like to play the Godfather."

Playboy: What?

"I went from being an eccentric runaway (to San Francisco) and offbeat filmmaker whose tastes ran to arty films that didn't make money, to one of the top five most sought after, highest-paid directors in the world."
— FRANCIS FORD COPPOLA

Coppola: It's true. He said, "Let's you and me buy this goddamned book and make it ourselves." I said, "Well, it sounds great, but ... "

Playboy: Why, in both *Godfather* films, are your female characters so submissive and acquiescent?

Coppola: That was how the women were represented in the original book and, from what I know, it was the role of women in the Mafia fabric. In *Godfather: Part II*, I was interested in developing a more contemporary, political view of women in the person of his wife, Kay, and in her symbolic statement of power when she had her unborn son killed.

Playboy: If Kay was such a liberated and defiant woman, why did it take her so long to leave Michael when she was no longer happy with him?

Coppola: It may seem like a long time, but actually they're together only six or seven years. How many people do we know who stay together unhappily for 15 years or more before they finally split? Also, during the '50s, there were a lot of forces that tended to keep men and women together way beyond the point when they should have parted. Think of how many husbands have kept their wives and held their families together by promising that things would change just as soon as they became vice presidents or had $100,000 in the bank or closed the big deal. I've strung my own wife along for 13 years by telling her that as soon as I was done with this or that project, I'd stop working so hard and we'd live a more normal life. I mean, that's the classic way husbands lie. Often the lies aren't even intentional. And it's easy to string a woman along for years by doing exactly that. Michael lies to Kay in that way and she believes him at first — because she wants to believe him.

Playboy: Why *do* people tend to get sucked in by their own lies? Do they just sell out to the system?

Coppola: Well, people like myself, who decide that it's necessary to work within a system in order to be able either to change it or eventually to go off on their own to subsidize the kind of work they believe in, inevitably become changed by the process, if they go along with it. I know a lot of bright young writers and directors in Hollywood who are very successful — some of them I gave jobs to four or five years ago — and they're making a lot of money; but they're no longer talking about the things they used to talk about. Their conversation now is all about deals, about what's going to sell and what isn't. And they rave about their new cars and their new $400,000 houses. They don't even see or hear the changes in themselves. They've become the very people they were criticizing three years ago. Like Michael, they've become their fathers.

Playboy: One last question: You have said you'd never make a *Godfather III.* But is the story of Michael Corleone really over?

Coppola: Nine times out of ten, people who say they're never going to do something wind up doing it. Right now, I don't want to make another sequel. But maybe 30 years from now, when I and all the actors have gotten really old, then it might be fun to take another look.

Page 386: Robert De Niro has little dialogue, and only a few lines in English, so he used his eyes and body language to communicate his thoughts.

Opposite: Together Mario Puzo and Coppola wrote the screenplays for the *Godfather* trilogy.

Page 390: Vito prepares himself mentally to kill Fanucci.

"You're Too Quiet For Your Own Interest"

"I was interested in the idea of succession —
showing a father and son both in their own
time and drawing a contrast."

FRANCIS FORD COPPOLA

"Both the Mafia and America feel they are benevolent organizations. Both the Mafia and America have their hands stained with blood from what it is necessary to do to protect their power and interests. Both are totally capitalistic phenomena and basically have a profit motive." —FRANCIS FORD COPPOLA

Pages 392–393: Vito Corleone, on the roof, tracks Don Fanucci below.

Pages 394–395: Fanucci strolls through the streets believing himself to be in control of the neighborhood.

Page 396: Vito waits patiently.

Page 397: Vito assassinates Fanucci.

Pages 398–399: Vito makes sure Fanucci is dead.

Above: Coppola helps load the bullets.

Opposite: Fanucci falls awkwardly in his doorway, caught unaware.

Pages 402–403: The celebratory fireworks are set off.

"You Can Never
Lose Your Family"

"God bless America. We're gonna make a big business!"

———◆◆◆———

GENCO ABBANDANDO

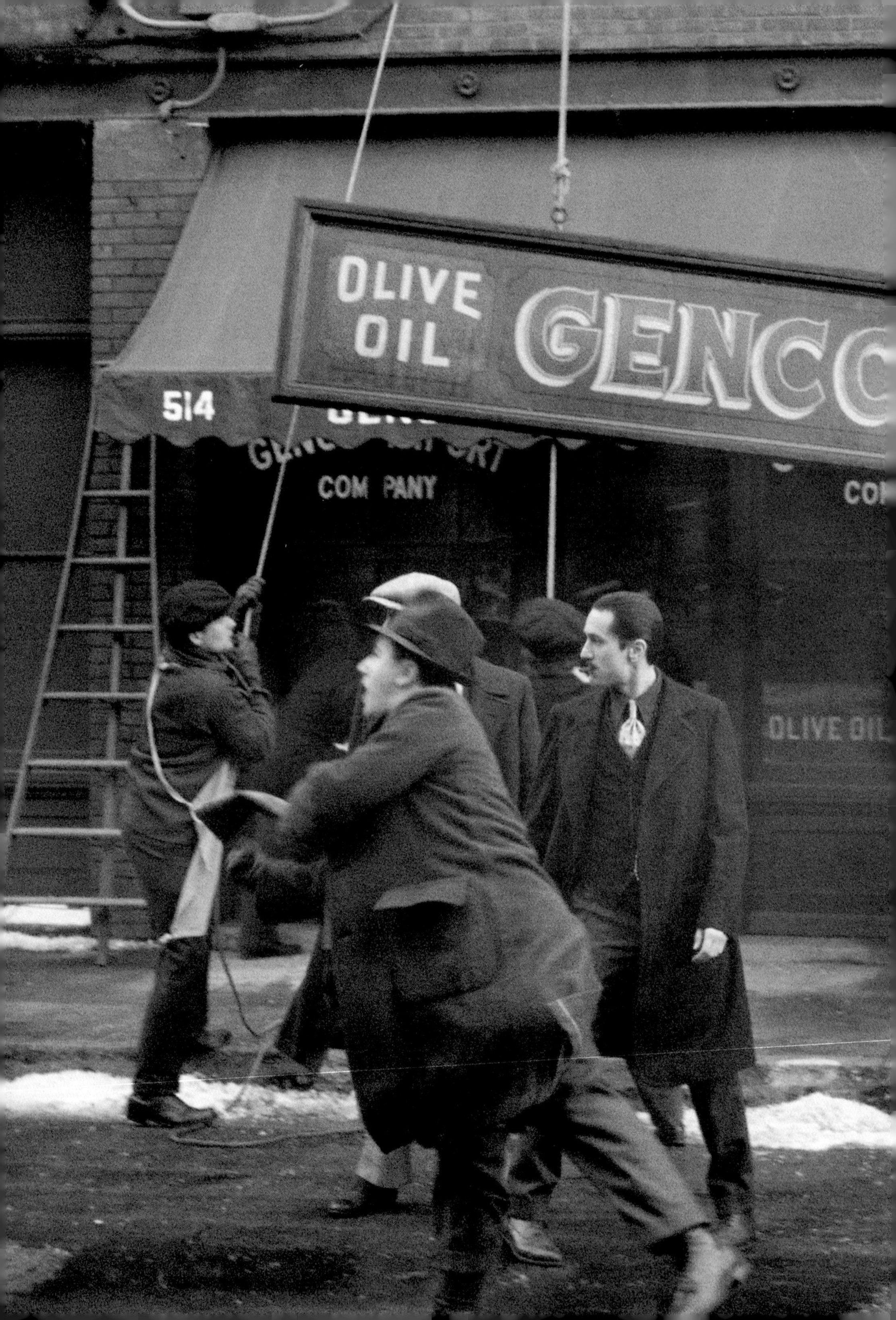
OLIVE OIL
GENCO
514
COM PANY
OLIVE OIL

Page 404: Don Vito is now a respected man in the community.

Pages 406–407: Clemenza, Don Vito, Genco Abbandando, and Hyman Roth (John Megna) in front of the new business enterprise Genco Importing Co.

Above: Beginning a long-lasting relationship: Clemenza, Don, and Sal Tessio (John Aprea).

Opposite: Echoing the opening scene of the first film, Don Vito with a cat.

Page 410: Michael brings Pentangeli's brother Vincenzo (Salvatore Po) over from Sicily as a reminder of the old codes of conduct.

Page 411: Frankie Pentangeli realizes that he must keep quiet.

"I think *The Godfather: Part II* is a more ambitious, serious . . . beautifully made film than any film this year."

— FRANCIS FORD COPPOLA

Pages 412–413: Michael Corleone comes under intense scrutiny by the committee, which consists of filmmaker Roger Corman, producer Phil Feldman, author Richard Matheson, and others.

Pages 414–415: Although she does not want to be there, Kay publicly supports Michael at the hearings.

Below: Michael reacts violently when he finds out Kay aborted their child.

Opposite: Kay and Michael divorced in 1959, after which Kay remarried. Michael thought it was in the children's best interests to entrust Kay with their education.

"I find it a great dishonor for me personally
to have to deny that I am a criminal."

— MICHAEL CORLEONE

"In The Name Of My Father, And My Brother . . ."

"Allow me the honor of introducing someone.
My partner in America, in New York. His name
is Vito Corleone."

DON TOMMASINO

Page 418: Visiting Corleone, Sicily: Mama
Corleone (Francesca De Sapio) with baby
Connie, Don Vito carries Michael, with
Sonny (Roman Coppola), Fredo in front.

Pages 420–421: Dining at Don Tommasino's
villa.

Pages 422–423: De Niro and Coppola enjoying the local produce.

Below: Robert De Niro playing with a child
between takes.

Opposite: Don Vito asks the children to
distribute gifts. Don Tommasino (Mario
Cotone) is at left.

"Even the strongest man needs friends."
—— MARIO PUZO

Opposite and below: This scene was deleted from the film.

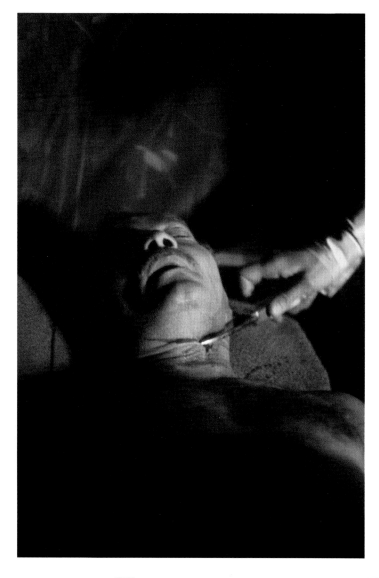

427

"If only we'd had another two weeks,
it could have been great!"

—— FRANCIS FORD COPPOLA

Opposite: Robert De Niro having fun
on the set.

"My dream of dreams was that *The Godfather* would net me $1 million, and that, conservatively invested, could bring around $50,000 a year, and with that coming in I could spend all my time writing my own stuff, without the interruption of having to deal with the studios." — FRANCIS FORD COPPOLA

Opposite: Francis Ford Coppola and his wife, Eleanor, with their young children Roman, Sofia, and Gio.

Opposite and below: Coppola, with his son
Gio at his feet and Robert De Niro looking over his shoulder, tries to find a quiet
moment during filming to read *Variety.*

Below: Don Corleone is an olive-oil importer, visiting Don Ciccio to ask for his blessing.

Opposite: De Niro visited Sicily for three weeks to research his role and learn the language.

"Most Italians who came to this country are very patriotic. There was this exciting possibility that if you worked real hard, and you loved something, you could become successful." — FRANCIS FORD COPPOLA

Pages 436–437: Don Ciccio (Giuseppe Sillato) learns that Don Vito is the son of Antonio Andolini just before he is killed.

Left: Don Vito and his family prepare to return to New York.

Right: Don Vito and his eldest son, Santino.

Pages 440–441: Don Vito bids farewell to his great friend Don Tommasino (Mario Cotone), who lost the use of his legs during the assassination of Don Ciccio.

"If History Has Taught Us Anything, It's That You Can Kill Anybody"

"This time I really set out to destroy the family. Yet I wanted to destroy it in the way that I think is most profound — from the inside. And I wanted to punish Michael, but not in the obvious ways. At the end he's prematurely old, almost syphilitic, like Dorian Gray. I don't think anyone in the theater can envy him."

FRANCIS FORD COPPOLA

Page 442: Don Michael orders the death of his brother Fredo because he betrayed the family.

Pages 444–445: The run-down Kaiser Estate at Lake Tahoe was renovated for the film, and provided a bleak background to a bleak film.

Opposite and below: Connie Corleone, dressed in mourning, after the death of Mama Corleone.

Pages 448–449: Hyman Roth is assassinated by Rocco Lampone (Tom Rosqui, right) at Miami Airport.

The Godfather Part III

"The Only Wealth In This World Is Children"

"A man like Michael Corleone, in every great tragic tale of kings and stuff, always has a part of him that is a sinner, that is evil, and another that is pure and innocent. The daughter symbolizes that, and, in the end, when he loses her, he loses that innocent, pure part of himself."

FRANCIS FORD COPPOLA

> ## "If you were raised as I was, everything you do is to make your family proud of you."
> — FRANCIS FORD COPPOLA

Pages 452–453: A portrait of the Godfather's extended family and friends: Top row: Father Andrew Hagen (John Savage), Johnny Fontane (Al Martino). Middle row: son Anthony Vito Corleone (Franc D'Ambrosio), Archbishop Gilday (Donal Donnelly), Don Michael Corleone (Al Pacino), daughter Mary Corleone (Sofia Coppola), Vincent Mancini (Andy Garcia). Bottom right: Don Altobello (Eli Wallach).

Page 454: Don Michael Corleone.

Opposite: Mary Corleone is the honorary chair of the Vito Corleone Foundation. She gives a check for $100 million to Archbishop Gilday for the resurrection of Sicily.

Right: Vincent Mancini flirts with journalist Grace Hamilton (Bridget Fonda), who is looking to interview Michael Corleone.

Pages 458–459: Johnny Fontane serenades Connie Corleone Rizzi, as he did on her wedding day.

Opposite: Michael is trying to extricate himself from the old business of violence.

Below: Joey Zasa (Joe Mantegna, right), accompanied by his bodyguard Anthony "The Ant" Squigliaro (Vito Antuofermo), comes to pay his respects to the Don.

Pages 462–463: Vincent, Sonny Corleone's illegitimate son, is supported by his aunt Connie.

"*The Godfather* isn't my life. I've made other movies."

— FRANCIS FORD COPPOLA

Opposite: Grace Hamilton spends the night with Vincent. When she wakes, she is held hostage by killers looking for Vincent.

Right: Vincent takes care of the killers.

"Just When I Thought I Was Out, They Pull Me Back In"

"I am not interested in the Mafia.
I do not like violence in films."

FRANCIS FORD COPPOLA

"Like all actors, [Pacino is] spoiled, he doesn't want to wake up in the morning, he's not comfortable, etc., but I always knew that the way to deal with Al is with his intelligence."

— FRANCIS FORD COPPOLA

Page 466: Michael is haunted by his father's past; a portrait of Don Vito hangs behind him.

Page 468: Michael hands out large checks to the Commission, a group of dons who invested in the Atlantic City casinos.

Page 469 and opposite: The dons are attacked and virtually wiped out.

Below: Vincent and Al Neri help get Michael out safely.

"Never Hate Your Enemies. It Affects Your Judgement."

"[I]t is a] story of business, of finance, and the higher levels of the finance in the world and what the real Mafia is: people in the world who run everything and have absolute power without having to account to anyone about it."

FRANCIS FORD COPPOLA

Page 472: Vincent is groomed to take over the Corleone family from Michael.

Pages 474–475: Michael arrives in Sicily, where he will hear his son sing at the opera.

Below: Director Francis Ford Coppola oversees the scene.

Opposite: Michael Corleone arrives at Don Tommasino's compound in Bagheria, Sicily. He is given a hero's welcome by the people.

"Your enemies always get strong on what you leave behind."

— VINCENT MANCINI

Opposite, right, and pages 480–481:
Francis Ford Coppola, Al Pacino, and
Andy Garcia work on a scene.

Page 482: Michael Corleone waits for Kay
at the train station.

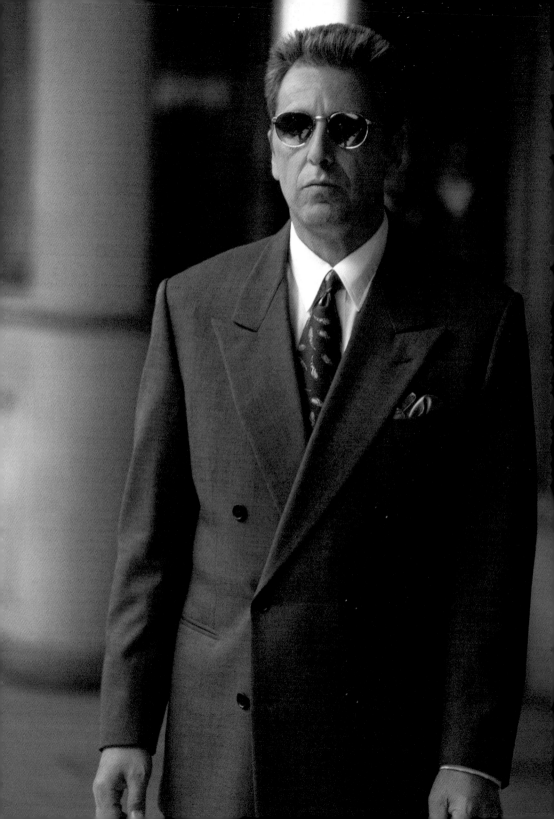

Every Family Has
Bad Memories

TEXT BY BARBARA GRIZZUTI HARRISON
EXCERPTED FROM *"GODFATHER III"* (*LIFE*, NOVEMBER 1990)

"Every family has bad memories," Michael Corleone says to his son, Tony, who rejects his father's murderous ways in *The Godfather: Part III.* "The father is a drunk, the mother is a whore. A son takes to drugs, somebody dies young of cancer, a child gets hit by a truck. They live in poverty, they get divorced. Somebody becomes insane. Every family has bad memories."

Taormina, Sicily. There is no sound in the courtyard of the Castello degli Schiavi (Castle of the Slaves) except for the insistent, thin, papery rustle of palm trees and the subdued swoosh of traffic outside guarded stone walls. Set among Mediterranean lemon trees and hot-pink bougainvillea, the miniature castle, silly and sinister, like a building in a fairy tale, looks as if it were dying from fungoid rot and mold. What those incised hooded eyes and curly ears on its aborted turrets symbolize in this land of abundant symbols no one knows. And yet for all its otherworldly loopiness, the 18th-century villa is familiar, as familiar as archetypal objects in dreams are familiar. I experience the mingled dread and anticipation of revisiting the scene of a blood crime that belongs not to the real events of the real world but to the world of real dreams.

Though I have never been here before I have been here before: This is the place where, in *Godfather I,* the beautiful young wife of Michael Corleone (Al Pacino) was blown up in a car, rigged by a rival Mafia family to kill the exiled son of Don Vito Corleone (Marlon Brando). I feel as if *Godfather I* and *II* are part of *my* history, *my* unconscious, vehicles for primary themes of good and evil (and family) and sin and redemption (and family) and communion and alienation (and family), of power and honor (and family). I am obliged to believe, so indelible are these films, that they are works of genius.

Which is the last thing Francis Ford Coppola, directing *Godfather III,* wants at this moment to hear. He seems determined to regard every compliment as a burden. It's not so much, one supposes, that he is exercising the artist's presumed prerogative to be perverse. It's

more probable that — behind schedule, over budget, beleaguered by Paramount to deliver a masterpiece by Thanksgiving (the new release date, for now: Christmas Day), his Zoetrope Studios bankrupt, faced with paying millions in disputed loans, subject to the caprices of actors who take themselves more seriously than God — he is very much as his wife of 27 years, Ellie, described him when he was filming *Apocalypse Now.* She said he was "beaten and tortured … depressed," waiting for the cathartic moment when the film is completed "to clarify and complete something within himself … feeling the power of being the creator-director and the fear of completely failing."

"It's just a *movie,*" he says. "You've been interested in *The Godfather* for a long time, haven't you?" he asks, distant, apparently bruised, as if my admiration for his work were a character flaw that worked to diminish him.

Well, I can't help it, I'm impressed, which has the effect of making Coppola belligerently defensive. "You want a scoop?" he asks. "I'll give you a scoop. I'm not all that interested in *The Godfather.*" Oh, dear. He is busily engaged in sawing off his own limb. Overhearing him, the Italian production manager smites her forehead and rolls her eyes to the heavens: Francis is a public-relations nightmare. "I hate gangster movies. I hate violence. This is not the real world. There's nothing romantic about this," he says and then, reversing himself, "Brigands are always romantic."

"It's impossible to talk about a movie after 106 days of shooting," he goes on, weary and irascible. He soliloquizes disjointedly: "I don't hang out with those guys, with mafiosi. Well, I used one Mafia guy in *Cotton Club.* He happened to be there; he seemed a plausible enough actor, so I used him.

"*Godfather* isn't my life," he insists. "I've made other movies." None of them has been blessed with the critical and commercial success of the 1972 and 1974 *Godfathers;* none of them has become so much a part of our culture. This rankles. He had a lot invested, personally and

> **"As in all classic stories, the daughter always represents purity, like Gilda in _Rigoletto_. I remember that when I was a child, I was always so heartbroken at the end of _Rigoletto_ because he lost his daughter, his only love."**
>
> — FRANCIS FORD COPPOLA

financially, in movies like _One from the Heart_ and _Rumble Fish_, and they were disasters. And now he talks some talk designed to prove that _Godfather_ isn't the be-all and end-all of his creative existence; it is not what defines him. "Everything I do I invest myself in. Moving a chair. That's a decision. Talking to you. Sitting in the shade …" And on and on. "When I was a kid I learned that if you didn't strike a diamond with one perfect blow, it wouldn't be perfect. I do that 60 to 1,000 times a day here — and each time it costs me hundreds of thousands of dollars.

"All of us operate out of fear and insecurity. Actors are relating to their insecurities, not to you. You learn to accept calls at 2:00 a.m. Actors are concerned with themselves, but directors have to be concerned with every detail — a director is a shrink, an uncle, and a visionary."

Coppola's vision for _Godfather III_ energizes the set in Sicily. The word _masterpiece_ is on everyone's lips; so is _Shakespeare_. Tension and exhilaration produce a monitored delirium. The crew and the actors are enlivened with the great expectations Coppola cannot quite disguise. He suggests that the themes of _Godfather III_ are the themes of _King Lear_; he and Pacino quote _Hamlet_ to each other. But it is _Lear_ they return to, again and again. When he does not know he is being observed, Pacino, an introverted man, dark and beautiful, claws at the sky, his mouth open in a soundless howl of rage. This is mighty Lear brought low, screaming at the heavens, betrayed and rejected by those he best loves and trusts, stripped of all that gave life and power and riches meaning, suffering

Above: Anthony Corleone (Franc D'Ambrosio) is a gifted opera singer.

the grief of a man whose child dies before he
does; and this is Michael Corleone, betrayed
and rejected, embodying the principle that
character is destiny, that men are destroyed by
their own actions.

"Do you love Michael Corleone?" I ask
Coppola.

"I *am* . . . I identify with him," he says.

His wife once equated Coppola's filmmak-
ing with a "personal journey into himself." And
though Coppola usually resists any psychological interpretation of his work, he did admit,
early on in the filming of *Godfather III,* that he
has "an uncanny way" of making movies that
reflect what's going on in his life.

Lear? Does Coppola now see his life in
terms of tragedy?

Those closest to him detect an abiding mel-
ancholy in the man, a grief that has not altogether
left him since Memorial Day 1986, when his
23-year-old son, Gian-Carlo (nicknamed Gio),
was killed in a motorboat accident. The son
idolized the father. He had quit school at 16 to
work at his father's side and learn how to make
movies, and he died before realizing his promise.
Changing the father forever.

Every family has bad memories.

Godfather III is a movie Coppola didn't want to
make. Paramount did — desperately. The first
two *Godfather*s won Oscars for Best Picture,
and together they have grossed an estimated
$800 million in theatrical, video, and televi-
sion revenues. But Coppola had vowed he was
through with the Corleone family, that he had

other movies to make. For years the studio
tried to develop a third *Godfather* without him
and, Hollywood being Hollywood, even considered using Sylvester Stallone and the expatriate
Russian Andrei Konchalovsky as directors.

When Coppola was at last prevailed upon
to make *Godfather III,* his need for money playing no small part in the decision, he holed up
with writer Mario Puzo and brainstormed and
gambled and wrote in the Peppermill Hotel
Casino in Reno. Six weeks later, they emerged
with a working script, and casting began. Pacino
was reportedly hired for $5 million, and Diane
Keaton got $2 million to reprise her role as Kay,
now Michael's ex-wife. Talia Shire (Coppola's
sister) was signed again to play Michael's sister.
The asking price of Robert Duvall, who played
the Corleones' *consigliere* in *Godfather I* and *II,* was
too high; he was written out of the script, and
John Savage was written in as his son, a priest.
The casting of George Hamilton as Michael's slick
WASP lawyer and financial adviser did not please
Paramount, but Coppola prevailed.

The production budget was set at $44 mil-
lion (and reportedly rose to $50 million), not
exactly chicken feed. But not, when fanatical
perfectionism is involved, a king's ransom either.
The color palette of the picture was of immense
importance to Coppola — and to Gordon Willis,
the cinematographer, and to Dean Tavoularis,
the production designer, who didn't, perfection
vying with perfection, always see eye to eye.
When the names Velázquez and Titian are used
to describe the look of a movie (burnished, deep,
rich, full, lush, velvety; moss green, burgundy,

claret, ocher, gold, dove gray, pearl), no detail is minor. Thirteen hundred carnations were thrown out because the color was wrong; Oscar-winning costume designer Milena Canonero's crew dyed hundreds of white shirts with Lipton tea so as to make them the proper ivory, not white.

The interior of the neoclassical Teatro Massimo in Palermo was recreated at Rome's Cinecittà studios. Over a period of 10 days, 23 minutes of the 69-minute opera *Cavalleria rusti-*

Keaton and Pacino were due to play a tender reconciliation scene between Kay and Michael, one can only assume that Coppola must have had to use all of his powers as "uncle" and "shrink" to avert disaster.

Then there was Winona Ryder, cast in the part of Michael's daughter, Mary, an Ivy League-educated young woman who handles her father's philanthropic affairs. Ryder came to Rome, couldn't get out of bed — nervous exhaus-

cana were performed for the cameras — Coppola will probably use 10 of those minutes. He even duplicated parts of the Sistine Chapel. Opera and religion: elements that ignite Coppola's artistic energy and inspire his legendary attention to detail.

At times the escalating budget seemed the least of Coppola's problems. In Rome, the offscreen romance between Pacino and Keaton suffered what one might politely call a sea change. Keaton issued an ultimatum to Pacino: Marry me when the movie is finished, or else. Given that

tion — and returned home almost immediately. Coppola raged at his producers; the production was plunged into turmoil. And then he came up with an idea that almost caused a revolt on the set and dumbfounded Paramount executives: He cast his inexperienced, 18-year-old daughter, Sofia, as Mary, who falls in doomed love with Vincent (Andy Garcia), the fiery bastard child of her uncle Sonny, Michael's murdered brother.

Two members of Coppola's family were now part of the cast — Sofia and Talia Shire, who, no longer a supplicant as she was in the other

Below: Preparing costume and makeup
for Talia Shire

Opposite: Kay arrives in Sicily.

Godfathers, plays a dignified, impressive matri-
arch. Actually, the cast includes three members
of Coppola's family, if you count a couple of lines
spoken by Coppola's mother, Italia, in a group
scene — for which, when I last saw her on the
set, she was vociferously demanding union scale.

The saga of the Corleones was becoming,
by degrees, the saga of the Coppolas.

Coppola "identifies" with Michael.

Godfather III is the story of an aging and diabetic
Michael Corleone's starved and desperate
desire for legitimacy and of his links to the
Vatican as the agency of his secular redemption.
It is also about power and succession, love and
betrayal, sin and absolution — and, above all,
family. The family as icon and reality. The family
as the source of joy, sorrow, deformity, and for-
giveness. There is nothing that is not contained
in the family, the institution to which, even if we
are not pledged, we are bound.

In a world ruled by a deadly code of honor
and tradition, family ties are never broken; the
connection may be a violent one, but it is lasting.

Coppola is obsessed with family. The source and the subject of his art is just that; Sicilian novelist Leonardo Sciascia calls it "the agonizing religion of family."

In *Godfather III*, Coppola also confronts the awesome power of the Catholic Church. And he goes far beyond an exploration of the materialism of religion: He taps into our experience of sin and our violently divided feelings about sin — its deliciousness, and our simultaneous need for absolution. He gives us the world, the flesh, the Devil, and God. And he gives them to us in the context of the family, from which we — and he — can never escape.

It is the 56th wedding anniversary of Italia and Carmine Coppola; coincidentally, Francis Coppola is filming a wedding scene in an exquisite little Baroque piazza just north of Taormina. Carmine's leonine head lolls, and he drops off to sleep as his son, in heavily accented Italian, directs Italian extras and bit players. Carmine snores. Italia prods him awake; his snores exasperate and shame her. He opens an eye long enough to tell her they don't embarrass *him*. It's hard to know where their real tenderness begins and their mock irritation leaves off. Italia is wearing tight black pants, a fuchsia silk blouse, a reversible Chinese jacket with a mandarin collar, men's brown polyester socks, and sling-back, patent-leather spike heels. She has lipstick on and bright-green eye shadow. She is 78.

While his mother and father play at quarreling, Coppola directs Keaton and Pacino, who have joined the wedding party and are dancing together. It's the kind of scene he does so brilliantly, the encapsulation of the intimate within the spectacular. When the scene is over, Keaton greets Italia and Carmine and says brightly: "Fifty-six years! How *did* you *do* it?"

Carmine: "I survived."

Italia: "Can you advise me what to do with this man?"

Carmine: "That's why men die younger. They work."

Francis: "What does that mean? She scrubbed the floors and washed and waxed and cleaned and cooked."

Italia: "And I survived because I said yes to everything — and kept the checkbook."

"I grew up very Italian-American, not like De Niro, who grew up American," Coppola has told me. He has been hearing these conversational feints and jabs all his life. He grew up watching domestic guerrilla theater, Italian-American style.

"I keep the books," Italia says. She is as talkative as her son now is taciturn. "My Carmine lost all his money on Wall Street. If it was up to him, we'd be living on potatoes and onions. I keep the checkbooks. I'm $7,000 away from 1 million."

Italia has taken a pointed dislike to one of Francis's assistants, who pays her little attention. "Who are these people who ignore me,

Below: Connie and Mary
at the train station.

can you advise me?" Italia keeps score of
slights; she is the caretaker of family grudges
and animosities. For example, she is vocally
indignant about relatives who "came out of
the woodwork" when "Francie" achieved fame,
even though "Francie" is eager to accommodate
them. "What am I, nothing? Francie wouldn't
be here if I didn't have him in my stomach.

"I'll tell you a story. One of Carmine's
brothers was in love with me too. He died. His
mother said, 'Good.' *Good?* Is that a way for a
mother to talk? She said it would bring dishonor
to the family if two men loved the same woman.
She shouldn't have worried. I wouldn't have
married him.

"Do you think Carmine should dye his
hair? What do you think? Can you advise me?

"I used to manage that man. I was his business manager. I gave it up. Enough's enough.
I made it work. I made everything work. I was
his legal secretary, and I made everything work.
Enough's enough.

"I was born in Brooklyn, at 525 Grand
Street, above the old Empire Theater. You know
that place? My brother was a trumpet player at
Radio City Music Hall when Carmine played in
the orchestra there. That's how we met.

"You know, he wanted to marry a beautiful
blond. But he hung around me. He got jealous
when I danced with someone else. So I said,
'Dance with your beautiful blond, Carmine.'

"They think the genius comes from
Carmine's side. If Francie hadn't been in my
belly, where would he be?

"My father gave Paramount Pictures its

name, did you know that? You didn't know
that. He brought American films to Italy. He
wrote Neapolitan songs. Yeah, they sang one in
The Godfather.

"What do men know? I love that Ellie, she's
a saint. I wouldn't put up with it. Even when
Francie was with That Other Woman, he loved
Ellie. And when That Other Woman wanted
him to leave Ellie, he wouldn't. Ellie — she
stayed and she gained."

"*Ma!*" Talia Shire seeks to stem the tide of her mother's confidences. (Francis is now watching his mother from across the piazza; he looks exasperated … amused … alarmed … resigned.) Talia, pretty, practiced in small talk, casually friendly, talks about her three children, about diets. She tries to shift the conversation into neutral, but Italia is undeterred: "Talia doesn't like hanging around the set when she's not working; she gets aggravated. Poor Francie, he works so hard. Yeah, Al's sweet to him. Except when he isn't sweet, then he's not so sweet. Everybody's got a temper."

The set is hushed when Coppola, big, bearded, sloppy, makes his entrance. He is followed by a pale old man who is chewing his cud, a shuffling old man whose feet look tired in their old-man's shoes, whose layered cardigans are hitched up in the back. Poor old man on a cane, head bowed, fedora dusty. "Shouldn't somebody get that guy off the set?" a photographer whispers. And suddenly there is a communal intake of breath: The old man is Pacino. He dies. For the first of several takes he enters death gently. His old hands peel an orange; his heavy head nods; and he dies.

Would the Angel of Death claim Michael Corleone — this man in whom family feeling and evil are so intimately braided — so softly?

On the next take Pacino slumps in his chair, loses his precarious balance, and falls, his face hitting and scraping the gravel, lifeless on the ground. Heedless puppies frolic over Michael Corleone's inanimate body. We are all frozen, motionless in the brilliant sunlight — and then Keaton swings her arms in a wide arc and applauds, breaking the spell and disrupting the magic.

The next day, on the *corso* in Taormina, a young antiques dealer remembers me from the set. "He doesn't really die, does he?" he asks anxiously. "It's a joke, isn't it? He doesn't die?"

I tell Pacino, who says: "Did he mean me? Or did he mean Michael Corleone?"

"I don't think he could tell the difference," I say.

"Well, I can't tell the difference either," says Pacino.

After five months of shooting in Rome and Sicily, Pacino finds himself in a neo-Gothic church on Mulberry Street in New York's Little Italy. As the choir from St. Patrick's Cathedral

"You don't have to confess your sins to a stranger."
— CONNIE CORLEONE

sings in a golden light, Michael Corleone, old and tired and ill, is knighted with the Papal Order of St. Benedict. There is a wonderful moment when handsomely dressed gangster Joey Zasa (Joe Mantegna) walks down the aisle, prepares to genuflect — and then turns first to hand his hat to his bodyguard. Even before God, the Mafia preserves distinctions of rank (this of course is heresy; it is the kind of detail only a director of Coppola's background and acuity would know to include).

There is a sense of work well done. Outside the church the actors congregate. George Hamilton in a cashmere coat, as tan as an ad for tan. Franc D'Ambrosio, who plays Tony, the son of Michael Corleone, wearing brown contact lenses to disguise his blue eyes. Mantegna, who plays Michael's most ambitious and dangerous rival, muses about the dramatic impact of the film: "We're drawn to Michael, but the end is devastation. There are no good guys here. There are only bad bad guys and good bad guys. The violence cancels out the warmth."

No, there is a warmth, an emotional richness in this story that nothing can eradicate. A quality of tragic grandeur, a heartrending recapitulation of *Lear*.

I think of Lear and his Cordelia when I see Coppola's daughter, Sofia, standing with the other actors outside the church, her eyes gentle and her handshake delicate. She says she was the baby who was baptized in *Godfather I* — in that dazzling scene when Michael Corleone stands before God to reject, on behalf of his godchild, the world, the flesh, and the Devil. And as Michael intones the holy, cleansing words, his minions mow down members of a rival family with machine guns. Images of blood and water. It was in this very church that the baptism took place.

Connections, connections. Coppola "identifies" with Michael, Michael is a surrogate for Lear. Coppola lost a son, Lear lost a daughter. I think about the ending of *Godfather III*, how closely guarded a secret it is, how Coppola has used words like "spectacular," "heartbreaking," and "tragic" to describe it, and I wonder: Why did Coppola replace Winona Ryder with his own daughter in the role of Michael's daughter? Must Michael suffer as Coppola has, so that Coppola, like Lear, may howl his private anguish to the world at large?

I have a sudden memory of Taormina and the courtyard of the pretty little church of SS. Trinità, where a Sicilian band was playing sweet, haunting music and giant red goldfish swam in a fountain. Coppola was using the Figli D'Arte Cutticio, a family of Sicilian puppeteers, in his wedding scene. Wedding guests watched while the splendid puppets performed, as large, almost, as life and more brazen.

The Sicilian *teatro dei pupi* derives from the Norman code of chivalry, which Sicilians, harshly and unjustly ruled, observed for many centuries. These puppets idealize the Crusades and celebrate the feats of Orlando, Charlemagne, the legendary King Arthur, and the Knights of the Round Table. Whatever form the story takes, the moral is always the same: A man's most sacred possession is his honor. To safeguard their honor and their property — including their families — Sicilian landowners hired armed men, governed by loyalty, austerity, and secrecy. They conducted their affairs violently, and in due time armies created in the name of family and honor became the societies called the Mafia.

In the story that the puppeteers were acting out, a young girl falls in forbidden love with a cousin, and to preserve the family honor the affair is brought to a tragic end.

Lear, Corleone, Coppola.
Every family has bad memories.

Opposite: Talia Shire as Connie Corleone Rizzi.

Page 494: Kay and Michael divorced in 1959, with Kay getting custody of Anthony and Mary. She has since remarried.

"I'm Not The Man You Think I Am"

"The Catholic religion has confession, where you can be redeemed for your sins. I thought that it was very powerful for a man to wish to be redeemed."

FRANCIS FORD COPPOLA

Below and opposite: Michael shows Kay
the real Sicily, and even the house where his
father, Don Vito, was born.

Pages 498–499: Filming the puppet show:
A father kills his daughter because she was in
love with her cousin.

Below and opposite: Francis Ford Coppola,
Al Pacino, and Diane Keaton filming in Sicily.

"You are the only one left in this family with my father's strength."
— CONNIE CORLEONE TO VINCENT MANCINI

Opposite: Connie proves to be a real power and becomes Vincent's counselor.

Right: Although Michael and Kay become close again, events drive them apart.

Pages 504–505: Michael gives all his power to Vincent, the new don.

Page 506: Michael Corleone, aged 77, in Sicily, still mourning the death of his daughter.

Pages 508–509: Francis Ford Coppola says goodbye to Michael Corleone, the character who is central to the trilogy.

Pages 510–511: Michael Corleone, 1920–1997.

"The Death Of Michael Corleone"

"I try always to do something that's a little beyond my reach, so that I'll try my best. Sometimes I fail. Sometimes I almost succeed, but I think this is what life's all about."

FRANCIS FORD COPPOLA

Unless otherwise noted, all texts are printed with permission
by the authors:

Mario Puzo, "The Making of Godfather," from Mario
Puzo, "The Godfather Papers and Other Confessions,"
G. P. Putnam's Sons, New York, 1972. Reprinted by permis-
sion of Donadio & Olson, Inc. © 1972 Mario Puzo.

Shana Alexander, "The grandfather of all cool actors
becomes the Godfather," from LIFE magazine, March 1972
© 1972 Life Inc. Used by permission.

Nicolas Pileggi, "The Making of The Godfather – Sort
of a Home Movie," The New York Times, August 15th, 1971
© 1971 Nicolas Pileggi.

Peter Biskind, "Making Crime Pay," Premiere, August
1997. Reprinted by permission of ICM (International Creative
Management) © 1997 Peter Biskind.

The Playboy Interview: Al Pacino, Playboy magazine
(December 1979) / © 1979 by Playboy. Reprinted with permission. All rights reserved.

The Playboy Interview: Francis Ford Coppola,
Playboy magazine (July 1975) / © 1975 by Playboy. Reprinted
with permission. All rights reserved.

Barbara Grizzuti Harrison, "Godfather III," from
LIFE magazine, November 1990. © 1990 Life Inc. Used
by permission.

EACH AND EVERY TASCHEN BOOK
PLANTS A SEED!

TASCHEN is a carbon neutral publisher. Each year, we
offset our annual carbon emissions with carbon credits at
the Instituto Terra, a reforestation program in Minas Gerais,
Brazil, founded by Lélia and Sebastião Salgado. To find
out more about this ecological partnership, please check:
www.taschen.com/zerocarbon
Inspiration: unlimited. Carbon footprint: zero.

To stay informed about TASCHEN and our
upcoming titles, please subscribe to our free magazine at www.taschen.com/magazine, follow us on
Instagram and Facebook, or e-mail your questions
to contact@taschen.com.

© 2022 TASCHEN GmbH
Hohenzollernring 53, D–50672 Köln
www.taschen.com

Edited by Paul Duncan/Wordsmith Solutions
Design by Josh Baker

Printed in Bosnia-Herzegovina
ISBN 978-3-8365-8064-9